PET LOGIC

See the world through your pet's eyes – and experience your
life through a beautiful new lens

Sweet Betsy –
from one animal
lover to another…
To many mindful
connections!
♡ Nicole

PET LOGIC

See the world through your pet's eyes – and experience your
life through a beautiful new lens

Nicole Birkholzer

Illustrations by Maura Condrick

PET LOGIC
See the world through your pet's eyes – and experience your life through a
beautiful new lens

Copyright © 2016 Nicole Birkholzer
Cover by Libby Kingsbury
Illustrations by Maura Condrick

Author photographs and Sammy (the goat) by Jeff Woodward, Scout (the dog) by
David Milos, Cookie (the cat) by Ivonne Senn

Published and distributed by Smart Cat Publishing
www.smartcatpublishing.com

Legal Deposit: February 2016

Library and Archives Canada

Bibliothèque et Archives nationales du Québec

ISBN : 978-1-987957-58-7

When we look beyond the common relationship between man and animal, where we don't just project our needs, knowledge, and love but instead consider the animal's perspective, we'll be shown a world that is nothing short of miraculous.

—*Nicole Birkholzer*

Ode to the Animals

You invited me to explore a world that went beyond my imagination, and yet… makes so much sense.

Contents

Foreword

When the student is ready, the teacher will appear.

—Buddhist proverb

That certainly was the case for me.

Growing up, I was an animal fanatic. In Germany, most children start out taking vaulting lessons to develop balance and confidence on horseback. At age five I began a vaulting program on a blue roan pony named Piccolo. Two years later I transitioned into regular riding lessons. At about the same time, I was hanging out at a local farm. I spent afternoons and weekends feeding calves, watching the silage process, and, most important, brushing cows. I still remember hopping on the tractor at four o'clock when the farmer and his sons drove to the cow pasture for the evening milking. While the boys fed the cows and the farmer milked, I took an old metal currycomb and a bristle brush and scraped patties off the cows' hide.

Something told me the cows would appreciate that someone cared about them beyond their milk, cared about their well-being.

My grandparents lived close by. Since I had no pets at home, I visited their house often, pretending their German shepherd was mine. It was clear: I was going to be a vet, a zookeeper for elephants, or a farmer.

None of those jobs came to fruition. I went into advertising. When the agency I worked at became part of a worldwide agency network, we had several clients that required us to conduct business in English. My English skills were sufficient for buying a muffin at the London airport but not for managing the creation of a print campaign for Crest™ toothpaste. I asked my boss if I could spend six months at one of our network agencies in the United States in order to improve my English. My boss said yes, and I never looked back.

From the moment I arrived in New York I was intoxicated. I couldn't wait to explore this fascinating city. And yet it also dawned on me that not only was I *in* New York, I was *alone* in New York. I didn't know anyone, and I didn't speak the language.

Though I wasn't aware of it until later, I learned two new languages during my first year in New York City.

Before I mastered English, I learned how to read body language, facial expressions, and energy. To express myself and to understand others was challenging. I had to decipher people's needs, intentions, and emotions in other ways. Until I learned to speak, write, and understand English, the reading of others became my main communication tool. That first year would prepare me for the work I would do later with animals.

Ultimately I did trade in my career as an advertising executive in order to work with horses and with children who experienced physical and cognitive challenges. Taking the role as director of a therapeutic riding center in Massachusetts, I turned a backyard operation into a state-of-the-art therapeutic riding facility that now serves hundreds of students each month.

Stepping into this world reconfirmed what I knew as a child: when I treated people and animals as equals— partner beings and soul companions—I was able to cultivate new ways of connecting and communicating with all living beings. Observing the physical and energetic expressions of my colleagues back in New York City had trained me to become acutely aware and to facilitate life-changing shifts for students with the most challenging disabilities.

In 2003, understanding the powerful role horses played in these life-changing shifts, I expanded my work and built my own coaching practice in my backyard. Together with my horses, I facilitated many sessions in which people from all walks of life—executives, homemakers, mothers and children—reconnected with their inner resources, bringing them back to their natural state of well-being.

At the same time, I acquired a barn cat. Inspired by her ability to show me the world through her eyes, I sent a story to a local newspaper. The editor liked it so much that I was offered a monthly column where I could share my perspective on our relationships with animals.

Of course I said yes and started writing under the header "Mindful Connections."

The intent of my column was to show readers how to look at things from their pet's point of view. I mused how different your dog would feel if you let her lead you on your daily walk instead of pulling her from shrub to bush. I shared how my horse Star taught me to mindfully groom him by paying close attention as he responded to my hands and brushes.

Those moments felt like little gems. When I was totally present with the goat, the horse, the cat, or the dog in front of me, I realized we were relating in a brand-new way. Wanting to feel this deep connection more often, I focused even closer attention on how I was communicating with my animals, and how they were communicating with me. Through observation I realized that we were both trying to get our ideas and feelings across to the other; we were both seeking a deeper relationship and understanding—and with this realization, mindful connections were established. By the time I started a blog to share my experiences with a larger audience, I noticed that the same principles seemed to prevail in building a meaningful connection with anyone at all. When I applied those principles consistently, my relationships with my pets and all other beings became richer and more rewarding.

A couple of years later, Jesse, an ancient draft horse in dire need of TLC, entered my life. He pressed me to trust my instincts so that together we could heal his aching body and soul. Inspired by Jesse's recovery, I distilled everything I had learned and practiced over a decade and a half into 5 Mindful Principles and the Mindful Connections Wheel©, a mindful communication and decision-making tool that is helping people across the globe make profound changes in their lives.

In the following stories I share with you the humble beginnings of my discoveries. This book is a collection of some of the most poignant—and at times surprising—insights into pet logic. My goal is to reveal the wisdom that lies within the four-legged and winged ones in our homes and backyards.

1.
A Brand-New World

We were putting the finishing touches on our brand-new barn. It was exciting to finally bring our three horses home, except for one thing—keeping horses in the backyard meant we were inviting rodents to the property too. By storing hay and grain in the barn, we were providing the critters with not only a great home but also an all-you-can-eat buffet. We needed a cat.

I went to the local feed store to check the bulletin board. Hopefully I could find a cat who preferred the outdoor life we had to offer. Among the signs about lost dogs and horse trailers for sale I found one reading feral kittens available. Dan, the store owner, explained that these kittens were found in an abandoned building next door. As tempted as I was to rescue one of them, it did not seem practical. I had absolutely no experience with cats, and although I wanted a cat who could handle the outdoors, taking on a feral one seemed daunting.

I explained to Dan what I was looking for: "The cat would live in the barn, where there's a heated tack and grain room; and I need a mouser." Secretly I had another wish list: female, black and white, independent, and over a year old. But I wasn't going to be picky. After I finished, a voice chimed in from behind me.

"Would you be interested in my barn cat?"

I turned around. A woman in her sixties explained that she had several cats living in her barn-turned-garage. One in particular was very unhappy with the situation. None of the cats were allowed to go outside because the property was on a very busy road. She assured me that this cat had her claws and would love an indoor/outdoor lifestyle.

Well, that was a start.

I asked the woman, who introduced herself as Lucille, for more details. "Her name is Cookie," she told me. "She's a black and white female, and she seems to be a hunter. Whenever she escapes outside she brings me back a mouse."

I was sold.

Then she added, "She is a bit vivacious at times." That stopped me for a second but did not concern me enough to keep me from making an appointment to meet the cat.

I called my friend Cindy, a cat lover, and asked if she would come with me. I needed some professional input.

When we arrived at the barn, we immediately recognized Cookie as the one cat trying to squeeze out the door while we were trying to get in. Once we entered the room housing the three cats, I understood why Lucille had called her vivacious. This kitty had found her audience, and within seconds she owned the room. She was playing and running and hopping and jumping. When we tried to pet her, she made herself available for a split second only to be off again for more playing and running and hopping. Yes, Cookie was spirited, and possibly putting on a show to convince us that she was the one.

That was fine with me. After all, I was not looking for another cuddle pet; I had a dog who fulfilled that need. I was looking for a mouser.

Cindy saw something totally different; she saw a cat with a great personality and the fierce spirit that makes cats so attractive to cat lovers. She looked at me and said, "You've got to take this cat, and if things don't work out, I'll take her. She is amazing."

Before making the final commitment, I wanted Lucille to see where the cat would live. It was important to me that she understood that I would provide Cookie with a safe home. However, allowing her to be outdoors could still get her into trouble. Cats need to hunt and explore, but by doing so they can also become prey for a fox or coyote. Lucille understood, and she approved of Cookie's new home.

Six weeks later the barn was finished and Cookie moved in.

Though I had a lot of experience with horses and dogs, I'd never had a cat before and wasn't sure what to expect. To me this was a new and challenging responsibility.

Thanks to Lucille I had the best support system. She decked me out with everything a cat owner needed and then some: a cat carrier, a bed, a food and a water bowl, a bag of her food, a litter box, litter, toys, and treats. I wondered if Lucille had realized how little I knew about caring for a cat.

But there we were, Cookie in a huge crate in the middle of the tack room and me on the outside looking in, not sure what to do except to open the door. It took Cookie a few moments before she sauntered out and started exploring the new environment. I left the crate in place for a few days, in case she felt safer crawling back into a smaller space.

During the first couple of weeks, I kept Cookie in the tack room. I understood from Cindy and Lucille that she would have to learn that this was her new home. So I put signs on the door and proceeded with caution when entering her new home. After several days I opened up another room used for workshops, so she could expand her environment and explore new territory. Step three of expanding her world was opening the door to the hayloft. She loved that. There she could hide and hunt.

After about four weeks I felt Cookie had accepted the barn as her home. She and I had bonded slowly by exploring each other's boundaries. I would pet her gently from her head toward her tail, and when my hand was around her hip she would turn around and hiss at me. Note to self: she doesn't like that. On the other hand, in the mornings, when I sat down in the tack room to journal about my new life that included horses in my backyard, Cookie often joined me, rubbing her body along my boots, jumping onto my lap, asking to be pet.

At times she would throw herself on the ground and roll around like a dog in the grass, or a horse after a sweaty ride. I took it as an invitation to pet her belly. She taught me quickly that it wasn't. Her claws came out, followed by a look of disdain before she jumped up and ran into the hayloft. Got it—I had misread that invitation.

A month into our relationship I decided it was time to open the door to the great outdoors. I was certain Cookie knew that the tack room was her new home and that she would come back to her food bowl after venturing out. When I finally turned the doorknob and pushed the tack room door open, Cookie strolled out, giving me the "it's about time" look.

Oddly enough, I felt like a mother seeing her kid go off to preschool. I heard myself mumbling, "Stay safe, come back, I love you, this is where your home is, don't forget ..." How could I have gotten so attached in merely a month? What if she became someone's dinner and disappeared?

I need not have worried—though she strode outside with confidence, the moment Cookie saw the first horse, she sped back into the tack room.

I was relieved. This was her new home!

How foolish I was to think that I would "hire" a cat for rodent control while providing food and shelter in exchange. I was in love! I wanted our relationship to be more than that of a provider and a mouser. I wanted to understand Cookie better and decided to pay close attention to learn how we could bond more deeply.

With the tack room door open, Cookie now joined me as I went through the daily barn routines. In the mornings when I walked into the barn to feed the horses, Cookie greeted me in the aisle. After feeding, I cleaned the stalls while Cookie supervised, sitting about six feet away from me intently observing. When I moved on to clean the paddocks, she came along as I pushed the wheelbarrow from manure pile to manure pile. I was surprised. This type of behavior was more like that of a dog. I had had no idea a cat would be interested in connecting this way.

Cookie paid close attention to my routines. She knew when I was near the end of the chores; only then would she ask for my attention. Like clockwork, the moment I swept the last shavings out of the barn aisle, she marched into the tack room, asking me to hang out with her. Not to pet her but to keep her company. So I sat on the steps to the hayloft and watched her eat. The moment I did, she purred, telling me I'd made the right choice.

It seemed that the more I opened myself up to her world, the more she was willing to show me.

Though we were doing great when we worked together at a distance, things were still a little rough when we got physical. The first time I decided to pick Cookie up, she lasted about half a second in my arms before she jumped down to the ground. It was clear; Cookie didn't like to be held. She was, however, always glad to hop onto my lap the moment I sat down, which I rarely did. Now I had a choice: in order to be closer to Cookie, I had to stop being busy around the barn and instead take a break for the simple and sweet sake of being with her.

In the evenings our routines were similar to the morning. I'd meet up with Cookie in the barn aisle; we'd feed the horses and pick up around the barn before heading into the tack room. She'd eat dinner while I watched or, occasionally, stroked her furry back with a brush. Once she was finished, I'd say "Good night" and "See you in the morning" before heading back to the house.

One night, as I was sitting in my living room, Cookie walked by on the other side of the sliding patio door. She took a quick look and observed the scene before meandering on.

A couple of nights later she appeared at the same door. This time she reached up on the glass and tapped it. After a few moments of tapping she started to paw the glass, scratching it without using her claws. At the first tapping I wondered if she wanted to come in, which was not part of our deal, and so I tried to ignore her. But when she persisted and attacked the window more frantically, I decided there had to be more to the story and went out to investigate. As I stepped off the porch, Cookie caught up with me in the driveway. She ran down toward the barn, part driven, part tentative, then stopped in front of the tack room door but didn't enter. That was curious. I entered the tack room hesitantly, not sure what to expect. When I got to the center of the room my eyes were drawn to the left and landed on a *huge* cat, who was comfortably squatting in Cookie's little house. The strange cat looked at me with a "What the heck are you doing here?" expression. I wondered the same. Where did this big cat come from, and how dare he take over my girl's room? Needless to say, I got the intruder out and Cookie moved back in.

Standing in the tack room that night, I contemplated how much this cat had changed my life. For the previous six months I had been Cookie's willful student, trying to understand how she thinks and feels. Now I realized she had scouted out the area around the house two nights before, taking in the scenery, understanding that I was sitting in that living room at night. Then, two days later, she sought me out and asked for my help when her space was intruded. This was nothing short of remarkable. I could only imagine how pleased she must have felt to have delivered her message and communicated with her human.

As I took one more look at her in her kitty house, I was so tempted to pick her up and hug her tight. But she had taught me well; instead, I gave her a gentle pat and said good night.

PET LOGIC

"RAISING THE ROOF"

2.
Finding the Healer Within

When Jesse, a thirty-two-year-old black Percheron, arrived at our place from a local horse sanctuary one Easter Sunday, he was in rough shape. Under his yak-like fur his hipbones protruded because he was so thin. Wandering across the rolling pasture, he was off-balance and extremely unstable. His eyes showed that he was withdrawn, and when I stood next to him, I felt very little energy emanating from him.

The director of the sanctuary told me that Jesse had endured a long career as a working horse. He had logged as a youngster and later drawn carriages loaded with tourists before eventually landing at the sanctuary. There he was happily cared for. But the competition for hay with the younger and stronger draft horses became Jesse's demise. Somewhere along the way he got hurt, resulting in his lopsided gait. So when the director asked me if Jesse could come to our farm for the summer to catch a break, I readily said yes.

Jesse settled into his new surroundings right away. The pressure was off, no one was harassing him, he had a field to himself, and his meals were delivered on time. Like clockwork he stood at the fence to receive his food. Once the meal was served, he dove in, ate for thirty minutes, and then parked himself somewhere in the pasture to rest until the next meal came around.

It was very hard to watch him retreat day after day, distancing himself from any interaction. A couple of times I took a brush to his heavy coat, but after a few minutes he walked away. *Too much, too soon,* he seemed to say. I respected his needs and left him alone. It was clear that Jesse simply wanted to savor the peace and quiet.

About three weeks after Jesse's arrival, two friends of mine asked if they could come visit him in the field and brush him. The weather had gotten warmer, and Jesse's long fur was trapping his body heat, causing him to sweat. Since my friends weren't using a halter and lead rope, Jesse would have the liberty to walk off if he was still not ready for a grooming session, so I agreed.

I was surprised to see Jesse sticking it out for a while. Curious to observe more closely how he felt being groomed, I joined them in the pasture. I was just in time to witness Jesse's first try at communicating with his new people. As the three of us moved around him, working the brushes across his massive body, he started to change body positions. At first I did not realize there was a method to his shifts. Both friends were on Jesse's left side, one at the shoulder, the other near the flank, while I brushed his mane with a hairbrush on his right side. When I got closer to Jesse's head, he tucked his nose toward his chest and turned his head toward me. I thought he wanted me to brush his face, and so I did. But he persisted, getting his head around my body so I was now standing on the other side of him, next to his neck. "I guess you want me on this side," I told him. "But there's no mane to brush. Do you want me to brush your neck instead?"

Within moments I found a tick on Jesse's neck, and right next to it, another one. "Oh, I get it," I said to him. "You wanted me to find the ticks." No sooner had I said this than Jesse turned his face toward me, showing me his left cheek. Right where the cheek and the muzzle met was another tick. One of my friends ran to the barn to get the tweezers, and when she came back down the path toward the pasture, Jesse started to walk toward her, seemingly knowing what was coming. He patiently waited for us to take off the biting bugs, and the moment the last tick was removed, he turned around and walked into the adjacent field to rest. He accomplished his mission; he had utilized us humans to remove the bothersome ticks.

I sensed this interaction had created an opening to a new level of communication. We had just proven to Jesse that we were good listeners; he could relay information to us, and we would hear him and act accordingly. In short, we'd shown him that we were mindful. I guessed that Jesse would now try more often, and to a greater extent, put his communication out to us. And as his primary caretaker, it was my responsibility to be present and available to keep the communication going.

My friends and I discussed how none of this would have happened if we had approached Jesse in traditional horseman fashion. He would have been either cross-tied or ground-tied during grooming, and neither would have given him a chance to move his body around to communicate. He also would not have been able to walk away once he felt sufficiently cared for. The latter was important information for me; today Jesse *wanted* to connect with people, but in a limited way.

Wanting to provide the best care, I was out to learn as much as possible about him so I could understand his needs and note his progress. This gathering of information required that I stay in the present, so I could observe without distraction. It also meant that Jesse would need to have the willingness and freedom to express his feelings.

That day in the field had been significant. From then on the channels of communication were open, and I felt it was safe to address Jesse's physical issues. I believed he would guide me as we took on his healing.

While I paid close attention to Jesse's need for space, concocting nourishing meals and providing companionship when he was ready to connect, in order to give his recovery added momentum, I called in the troops of wellness practitioners, who could offer help in ways I couldn't.

The initial care for Jesse was challenging. Old injuries to his right hip caused him to carry his right hind leg far underneath his body, leaving him extremely unstable at the walk. He was also still underweight and therefore weak.

My friend Eve, a chiropractor for humans and animals, offered her unique, gentle, hands-on approach to healing. Her treatment releases blockages in the nervous system so that the connection between the body and brain via nerves is restored. As a result, patterns of stress and tension that cause disease are shifted. As the nervous system regulates itself, the body is often brought back into alignment. Then horses can experience increased oxygen and blood flow, better range of motion in stiff joints, and improved appetite and digestion.

Though I was a regular patient of Eve's and had experienced many of the benefits myself, I was stunned to see what her treatment did for Jesse. As Eve addressed different parts of his body, I saw how Jesse shifted himself back into alignment. Within four treatments his hip was back in its correct place and remained there.

In addition, our neighbor Lisa came every other day for a week, bringing crystals and flower essences to enhance Jesse's healing and lift his spirits. All the while, I provided him with an ever-changing, comprehensive diet, which brought him as much nutrition as he could process with his worn molars.

Through Jesse I learned that it can take a village to provide the best and most holistic care for our horses. Everyone was rooting for him. Offering our combined skills, we gave Jesse the treatments and attention that promoted his recovery. And his transformation became nothing short of magical.

A month after his arrival, Jesse, the horse who had been in danger of falling over at the walk, came trotting up to the fence to get his breakfast.

It appeared that somewhere between finding the ticks and straightening out his body, Jesse promoted me from lunch lady to napping buddy.

When I was out in the barn or fields to pick up manure, Jesse looked for me, parked himself at my side, shoulder to shoulder, then dropped his head ever so slightly, closed his eyelids halfway, and napped. I felt honored to be deemed trustworthy enough to watch his back. His naps were short, usually between five and ten minutes. When he woke up, he gave me a nudge with his nose, which I took as acknowledgment of time shared, and then he walked back into the pasture to graze near the other horses.

Next, Jesse allowed me to take a brush to his mammoth fur. It was obvious he liked the attention now. As I brushed his itchy body, he reciprocated by grooming me back, rubbing his wiggly lip on my upper arm. With a little elbow grease and some patience, he was shed out by the end of May. I considered the release of the hair part of his healing process, shedding the past and revealing a healthy coat underneath.

These interactions marked another big shift in our relationship. Next step: barn buddies.

Jesse repeatedly waited at the gate for me to walk out the back door and head to the barn. While I cleaned the stalls, he hung out with me, and then followed me around the fields on my daily search for lost fly masks.

Three months after Jesse's arrival, he was a different horse. His weight was up, his eyes sparkled, and his personality and charisma truly shone. I could finally see the proud and majestic carriage horse he once was.

Inspired by Jesse's remarkable recovery, I contemplated how others might become aware of the diverse holistic services available for horses. It could make such a difference for other horses too. Excited by that vision, I put together an educational event that offered a platform for equine-wellness providers to share innovative services and products that are proven, natural, and healing. The event was a celebration of the body, mind, and spirit of the horse, as well as of the people who dedicate their lives to helping horses stay well and happy. The horse sanctuary helped with the organization and was also the recipient of the monies raised.

I imagine Jesse had no lofty aspirations the day I met him. He wanted plenty of food, peace, and quiet space to heal. And I simply wanted to help him recover his body, mind, and spirit. But suddenly he was the inspiration for an event that would touch the lives of many people and horses alike.

Around this time we rescued an older goat named Marshmallow and a sheep named Isaac who had been headed for the auction. The day they arrived we led them into the backyard while Jesse rested in a field out of sight of the barn. As I settled them in, I recognized that it was a less-than-perfect time to be adding new members to the family. My time was limited, the equine-wellness event was only a few days away, and Marshmallow and Isaac needed a place to sleep. The extra stalls would have to be cleaned out and set up, which I wouldn't be able to do before the event. Eventually I decided to take a few portable fence panels and set up a makeshift stall in the indoor riding arena. At night I would close the big sliding doors so Isaac and Marshmallow would be safe from coyote attacks.

That arrangement worked well. In the morning I brought Mellow (our new nickname for her) and Isaac out to the pasture. At night they came back indoors. A few days later we were hit with a rainstorm. In order for Isaac and Mellow to have both access to the pasture and cover from the rain, I decided to give them free access to the arena and the pasture.

That very day Jesse decided to claim the indoor arena as well. Wanting to get out of the rain, he stood at the gate, asking to come in. I obliged; it was about time for him to meet our new family members.

While Jesse moseyed over to the arena, I continued to clean the temporary goat and sheep pen. Moments later, as Jesse rounded the corner, his confident stride came to a screeching halt when his eyes fell on Mellow and Isaac. He did not move a muscle. "Jesse," I said cheerily. "These are our new family members, Isaac and Mellow."

Jesse's response was shocking ... and instantaneous. He moved his right hind leg toward the midline under his belly and dropped his hip out of alignment. He stood frozen like that for a few moments, then turned and proceeded to gimp back through the arena door toward the gate, looking as bad as he had the day he'd arrived.

Watching Jesse head back to the barn was upsetting. His response to seeing Isaac and Mellow was so dramatic, I understood he must have had a bad experience with goats or sheep. What a setback.

My choice to rescue yet another animal—in this case two—had triggered some old fear in Jesse, and I needed to remedy the situation.

One thing was clear: Mellow and Isaac were not going off to the auction, and Jesse was not going anywhere either. I had to figure out how we could all live in peace. To start,

I'd keep Jesse and the ruminants apart. And I called Eve; Jesse was going to need more treatments.

Eve came the next day and was equally shocked to see Jesse's condition. It seemed he had lost all the progress he'd made. Thankfully, after only one treatment, Jesse was in much better shape. After Eve's second visit a few days later, Jesse was back to normal.

Jesse's quick recuperation a few days before the equine-wellness event reinforced my belief that people had to know about the amazing holistic equine practitioners we had in this area. The event turned out as I had hoped. It was an opportunity for horse owners and equine-wellness practitioners to connect over the healing of horses. And we raised some money for the sanctuary as well.

The day after the expo I finally had some downtime and decided to hang out in the barn. I grabbed the mounting block, put it next to the door, and looked around. The barn kitty was rolling in the sun, and Isaac and Mellow were napping behind me. This was the first time since their arrival that I could actually "meet" them. They were both still very shy and anxiously exploring their new environment and people. For now I figured I would simply be with them, letting them get used to my energy.

About fifteen minutes later, Jesse came around the corner, wanting to join me in the barn. Before I could interject, he stepped through the doorway. When he saw Isaac and Mellow, his hip immediately dropped out of alignment and his right hind leg found its way back under his belly.

"Oh no!" I called out. "This is crazy!"

Maybe crazy, but it was also true. Jesse was once again triggered.

Suddenly I had a sense about what he was afraid of. Over the last few months I had fed him separately from the other horses, and he relaxed, feeling that nobody was going to take anything from him. These new animals seemed to threaten his sense of security.

I walked up to his right hip and reached around his massive back end. "Jesse, I will take good care of you," I told him. "You will never miss anything. We love you, and we have enough love for all the animals and people on our property." I took a deep belly breath. "You are so important to me. I don't want anything bad to happen to you. Ever!" I looked at his face. "These two were in need of a home, and we could provide it. We will take good care of them, and we will always take good care of you, too. You will not miss anything because of them." I finished with, "I love you. Please bring your leg back into place and straighten out your hip." Then I stepped away.

After a breath or two, Jesse slowly moved his right hind leg back into its normal position. And his hip popped back into place and stayed there. Was it possible? Had I literally talked the trigger response out of him?

A few days later I stopped by the horse sanctuary to drop off a check. Of course I had to tell the director about my latest experience with Jesse. I didn't expect her to know if Jesse had ever had a traumatic experience with a goat or sheep. Jesse was over thirty years old, and he'd only been at the sanctuary for less than two years. He had lived a lot of life we knew nothing about.

When I got to the point in the story where Jesse had first noticed the goat and sheep in the arena, causing his hip to collapse, the director said, "Wait, now I remember about a year ago we had some crazy goats here at the farm. Someone dropped them and ran. They were really terrible. They got into everything, especially the feed buckets while the horses ate. They were so obnoxious, we had to find them a new home."

Mystery solved. Jesse had been terrorized by a bunch of goats that had robbed his feed bucket. The director and I concluded that in one of the food struggles, Jesse had possibly gotten injured, resulting in his bad hip. When I got back to the barn I told him I understood his fear and promised him that I would keep the goat and sheep away while he ate his grain in the morning and at night. That seemed to be all he needed to hear. During the day Mellow and Isaac joined Jesse in the barnyard and the surrounding pastures, and his hip stayed in place.

He had found his power again. When the ruminants tried to approach his hay pile, Jesse told them to back off, flattening his ears and showing his teeth. As upsetting as the situation initially was, in hindsight I realized that it all had worked out for the better. What appeared to be a disastrous choice, adding a goat and sheep to the herd, turned out to be blessing. Together Jesse and I not only worked through the old trauma but we went beyond it.

PET LOGIC

"CATITUDE"

3.

Beating the Baby Blues

Inspired by a bulletin board flyer I spotted at a local store, I decided to volunteer at a nearby wildlife rehabilitation center. The rehab needed short-term help with orphaned raccoon babies. Their mothers were usually killed by a car, a gun, or an arrow. The little critters needed to be bottle-fed, their cages cleaned, and their heating pads microwaved to keep their bodies warm and snuggly.

A couple of years earlier I had gone through two miscarriages. Though I had made peace with not being a mother, occasionally I felt a strong desire to nurture; helping orphaned baby animals seemed like the perfect solution to feed their needs as well as mine.

The volunteering required a six-month commitment. The raccoon babies usually arrived in the spring and needed to be fostered until the fall when they were ready to be released into the wild again. The chores varied. Early in the season most of the babies were only a few days old; they needed formula, their bellies rubbed to get their digestive tract working, and their bottoms cleaned because they couldn't yet take care of themselves. Within a couple of months they started to use a litter box and we introduced them to dry dog food, cereals, and vegetables. Often the babies had a sibling or two they got to cuddle up with. Any single raccoons were eventually introduced to one of the packs for socialization. Around eighteen weeks of age, the babies were transferred into outdoor cages, where they got exposed to wind and weather, preparing them for their future in the wild.

One day, after completing my chores with some of the younger ones, I decided to sneak in a quick visit with the adolescent raccoons in the outside cage before heading home. These were the orphans we had bottle-fed for two months; now they were three months old and grouped in a pack of four. At this age they were as entertaining as they were cute.

When I approached the door to the large, walk-in cage, the raccoons started to stir from their naps. Once up and going, all four of them ran toward the entrance and started to climb the wire-mesh walls. Since their cage had just been cleaned and hosed down, there were no dry spots where I could sit. I looked around for something that would suffice as a seat, and my eyes fell on a pink milk crate leaning against the side of the enclosure.

As I entered the raccoon condo—milk crate first—eight little paws grabbed and pulled on the bottom of the crate, guiding me to put it on the concrete floor. Following their direction, I placed the crate and quickly sat down before it became raccoon occupied. The little guys were beyond excited. Each little raccoon started to investigate every inch of the milk crate and me. We had become the new jungle gym on the playground.

To my right, someone was sticking little fingers into the fold of my capri jeans. On the left, someone had fingers in my clog, under my heel, peeling off the insole. Right behind me, someone was fingering my belt loops and eventually the elastic of my underwear. I couldn't move my hands and feet fast enough to keep the little investigators out of my personal "do not enter" zones.

In the midst of this, the fourth raccoon, a little female, climbed up the front of the crate and nestled into my lap. From there, she stretched her arms high and stroked my neck and chest. Now I turned to her and scratched her back, right above her tail. That spot was not only a favorite of most dogs but also loved by the raccoons. I could tell the little girl enjoyed the attention a lot, and she returned the favor by giving me little grooming nibbles on my arm.

There I sat, my clog halfway pulled apart, chew marks on the hem of my pants, and a fuzzy fur ball in my lap.

My moment of bliss was interrupted when the little female decided to leave. She climbed down the front of the crate, headed over to her food bowl, grabbed a golf-ball-sized cereal ball called "monkey chow," turned around, and climbed back onto my lap. There she wriggled herself once again into the perfect snuggle position and happily munched away. She quickly fended off any and all attempts from her pack mates to interfere with her cozy arrangement.

It was quite remarkable; in this moment all had come full circle. I was able to provide comfort and safety, and in return I received a feeling I had craved for so long but never experienced. I was answering a need for this raccoon baby and she was also answering mine. I was both giving and receiving affection. For someone who wasn't blessed with children, this was heaven. Absolutely heaven.

PET LOGIC

"APPRECIATION"

4.
Phoenix Rising

A while back, I consulted with a family in Connecticut who, over the previous two years, had rescued four draft horses, one Thoroughbred, and a donkey. A few of the equines came from auctions, while the others were rescued from backyards and riding schools. Both Holly and her husband Chris were relatively new to horses, but they intuitively provided a wonderful environment for their herd, with twenty-four-hour turnout, run-in shelters, an unlimited supply of hay, and barefoot trims. Holly and Chris were looking to eventually get the drafts back to work and the Thoroughbred under saddle as soon as each horse had recuperated from their physical, mental, and emotional wounds.

Holly had done her best to get a handle on the condition of each horse. She had researched each horse's history and keenly observed their behavior as individuals and as a herd. Her interpretation of the information she had collected and her own gut feeling suggested that several horses were ready to connect more deeply with their new people. What she now needed was a way to use the information she had absorbed to facilitate further connection and healing.

After I arrived at the property, Holly walked me out back to the large turnout where the herd was eating peacefully from a sweet-smelling round bale. The first horse who came to greet us was Phoenix, the beautiful copper-colored Thoroughbred Holly and Chris had rescued a year before. Phoenix's former life had been a far cry from the one he now inhabited. Raced at the track and eventually trained to become a school horse, Phoenix had been beaten literally and figuratively, and his body and spirit bore the scars. When Holly met him at a local boarding and lesson barn, he was rearing in the crossties and nipping and striking at any human coming too close—obvious signs of an unhappy, angry, and fearful horse.

Holly and her family took Phoenix to their farm and provided him with a safe and nurturing environment. And most importantly, other than occasionally attempting to groom him, they let him be. When Phoenix approached me, he seemed curious. He sniffed my hand and allowed me to stroke his forehead. I made a few attempts to touch various places on his body, but each time he walked away.

It was clear that touch, anywhere other than his forehead, was off-limits.

"That's one of the reasons I asked you to come," Holly said. "We interact with our horses mostly at liberty. Finally Phoenix is starting to seek our companionship, but every time we want to brush or pet him, he shies and walks away."

Holly thought that for Phoenix any kind of touch—brushing, scratching, even petting—elicited fear of what would come next: another ill-fitting saddle? The whip? And she was probably right. Although horses live in the now, a raised arm or the sight of a whip can trigger a memory of a painful or cruel experience.

However, trying to convince Phoenix that touch need not mean pain by continuing to touch him, even in the gentlest way, created a barrier to change.

"Why does Phoenix *need* to be touched?" I asked.

Holly thought for a moment. "I guess I want him to know that touch is good."

Chris had joined us at this point. He added, "Yes, as humans we express our love through touch."

"That's true," I said. "But what if loving Phoenix means *not* touching him?"

This thought was a revelation for Holly. As an equine massage therapist, Holly helps horses through touch.

"For Phoenix, touch has no positive associations," I said. As hard as it might be for us not to project our own experiences onto the horse, I explained, we had to accept the information Phoenix was providing us with as his reality.

Intrigued by our conversation, Phoenix had wandered back to our little group. I suggested that Holly locate Phoenix's "bubble," that invisible circle of personal space that surrounds every being and when breached signals danger.

While Chris attended to some of the other horses, Holly and I put our attention toward Phoenix, watching his facial expressions and body language to see at what distance he was comfortable with us and at what distance he considered us a threat. We stood about ten feet away from him, then took the first step toward him. Then we took a second step and a third. At seven feet he turned his head away from us, and we stopped immediately. Our goal was for him to be comfortable. We did not want him to walk off. I felt we were a touch too close and asked Holly to join me and back up half a step. Now Phoenix relaxed; his head dropped and he took a deep breath. He was comfortable with about seven feet of distance between us.

Having determined Phoenix's personal space, I suggested we "be" with Phoenix from this position. Holly and I faced his belly, staying behind his shoulder, allowing room for him to leave if that's what he wanted to do. We took several deep breaths and sent him thoughts of love, respect, and understanding. We told him silently that we would accept him for who he was and provide what he needed.

Within moments Phoenix closed his eyes. Holly and I could *feel* him relax, become contented and able to rest while his humans watched his back. Phoenix needed us to honor his personal space and to respect the fact that he did not want to be touched right now.

My sense was that respecting Phoenix's boundaries would allow for a huge shift in his perception of people. Traditional thinking might suggest that this horse needed to be "sacked out," touched over and over with hands, brushes, flags, and other seemingly scary objects until he became used to the assault. I explained to Holly that while that method could get the horse to surrender to being touched, it would not motivate him to reach out for touch on his own.

By giving him space, we were creating the possibility for Phoenix to reach out to Holly and her family, in his own time and on his own terms.

A few minutes later, Phoenix woke up, blinked, and then walked back to his herd mates. Our work with him was done.

A week later Holly reported the following:

You hit the nail on the head with Phoenix. He's a different horse. He knows we heard him. Yesterday, as I groomed Clay, one of the Belgian drafts, Phoenix came over, rested his head next to Clay's croup, and stood there until I was done. Occasionally he even bumped the brush in my hand! I asked him if he wanted to be brushed and then gave it a try … and he stood there and let me brush him! He let me curry him! It was a total transformation!

Two weeks later she wrote:

Phoenix and I groomed for a good twenty minutes. Whenever I stopped, he nudged me to continue. Every time I thought he was done and I walked away, he'd follow me. His head was by my thigh and he kept bumping me, so I started massaging him around his head. It feels like he finally surrendered, and now he can't get enough. Nicole, every time I'd try to stop he just kept asking for more. It was amazing, an incredible breakthrough. There were no walls, just total openness.

PET LOGIC

"SQUEEEEZE"

5.
When the Time Is Right

As we often did, my husband and I had stopped at the local farm stand in the morning for a cup of coffee. We were discussing the beautiful fall weather with other locals when a green pickup truck with an aluminum cage on the bed drove into the parking lot. The contraption on the back seemed unusual, and when I looked more closely I noticed two little noses sticking through the aluminum slats. Maybe it was a form of transport for miniature horses? The driver, a woman in her fifties, had grabbed a coffee and was now chatting with one of our friends a few tables over. Several times I tried to get the lady's attention so I could ask her what kind of animals she had on the back of her truck. After several failed attempts, I gave up.

My husband, who had seen my efforts, projected his voice and said, "My wife would like to know what kind of animals you have on your truck? Miniature horses?"

The woman turned her head slowly toward us. "It's a goat and a sheep," she answered, and I saw tears welling up in her eyes.

Her friend jumped in, asking, "A goat and a sheep? Where are you taking them?"

Now the tears started running. "I can't even talk about it," the woman answered. "I'm taking them to the auction. I kept them as long as I could, but the time has come …" Her voice trailed off.

I was moved and ready to jump into action. "Can I see them?" I said.

Another friend spoke up: "Nicole, you've got to take them. Save the goat and sheep." Then he looked at my husband. "John, come on, it's her birthday!" Which it was. "What a perfect gift for her!"

With the woman's permission, I walked outside across the parking lot, eyeing the two little noses sticking through the slats. Looking beyond the slats, I could see that the goat was white and surprisingly fuzzy. The sheep was brown with a classical Roman nose. He was breathing heavily, as though hyperventilating. John had followed me outside, and as the two of us stared at these creatures, we felt the same sense of urgency. The woman joined us and gave us a few more bits and pieces of information about the two.

She'd had them for nine years, had raised the sheep by hand and gotten the goat when she was about three years old. The goat was an Angora; the woman was a spinner and had spun their wool into yarn. She hinted that she was faced with a major life change and couldn't keep any of her animals anymore. She had found homes for the horse and cows, but nobody had offered to take in Marshmallow, the goat, and Isaac, the sheep. How could we say no?

Ten minutes later the goat and sheep walked down the plank from the truck bed into our driveway. I used a couple of fence panels to create a little pasture in our backyard. When the woman saw where her babies were going to live, her tears kept on rolling. Just this morning she had decided that today was as good as any day to take them to the auction. She had cried from the moment she left her driveway to the time she stopped to get a coffee. She could not believe that her trip had a happy ending.

As promised, the woman came back a few hours later, dropping off some grain, a pair of shearing scissors, and two skeins of yarn that she had spun from Isaac's and Marshmallow's wool. She was elated. A few days later we got a thank-you card, the name and phone number of the man who could shear them, and an invitation to join her spinning group.

Our horses were surprised when they took a look at these new creatures, and inspired to run across the pasture, heads high, snorting.

Both Marshmallow and Isaac were considered elderly. While Isaac's only problem was anxiety over separation from his former owner, Marshmallow had some other issues. She moved around so slowly that I renamed her Mellow, because she was. This was in part due to her age and in part because of her hooves. They were fairly overgrown and caused her to walk on the outside of her hoof walls rather than her pads. In my research I learned that ruminants' hooves usually get trimmed twice a year; we noticed soon, however, that her feet required trimming every two months and suspected that they hadn't been kept up with regularly.

The malformation created a lot of discomfort. At times Mellow would take a stance like a horse with laminitis, shifting the weight off her front hooves, carrying it instead on her hind end. It was hard for me to watch, but for the most part she was in good spirits, and when she wasn't I gave her the prescribed dosage of aspirin to ease the discomfort.

The following spring I noticed Mellow had lost a lot of weight. Despite her still "wearing" her winter coat— Angora and Kashmir goats, like sheep, need to be shorn every spring—she was looking pretty thin. In addition to her pasture meal of grass and dandelions, I added fat to her diet and fresh dark greens such as kale, lettuce, and chard. But she kept skipping her grain. In the back of my mind I started to question: When is pain too much pain? When is skinny too skinny? When was it time to release her?

Then, on one of those very warm summer days, I found Mellow lying on her side in the high grass of a pasture. She was breathing heavily and could not get up by herself. As soon as I helped her up, she collapsed again. Since she couldn't stand on her own, I carried her to the barn and placed her on the cool cement floor. I thought it was time to call our vet when suddenly Mellow moved her legs in an attempt to get up. I helped her onto her feet, and as soon as she was upright, she walked out the barn door to the closest patch of grass and started eating. Puzzled, I watched her for a while, but nothing indicated that she was ready to leave this world.

When the vet came to trim Mellow's feet, he gave her several vitamin shots, in hopes that it would boost her energy. And it did, though she did have days when she rested in the barn all day and hand feeding her was the only way to get her to eat; other days, she dove into her soaked hay cubes and went grazing around the property.

When the sheep shearer came late in the summer to give Isaac his second clip, I picked his brain, hoping he knew tricks of the ruminant trade that would help strengthen the little goat. He simply said, "She is an old goat." He also told me the story of the 103-year-old fellow living in a nursing home who had been required to drink energy drinks to keep him going.

I got it. The goal was not to prolong Mellow's life; my job was to pay close attention and notice when the time had come.

A few days later, after feeding her breakfast, I spent some time brushing Mellow head to toe. I paid special attention to how she felt, and to me she seemed content. For the rest of the day she rested on a bed of hay in the barn, which was just as well, since a rainstorm was moving in.

In the early evening, when I went out to feed the horses, Mellow was missing. I searched the barn, each stall, under the staircase, but Mellow was nowhere to be found. Now I started to worry.

She was such a timid mover. Had the horses run her over when they came up to the barn for dinner? Was she caught outside somewhere in the rainstorm? I went out to the search the pastures, the path to the pond, and the indoor arena but came up with nothing. Scanning the property one more time, I suddenly saw a white patch in the wet grass, wiggling and twisting. I ran across the pasture calling, "I'm here, Mellow! I am coming!" She responded with a mere little "mehhh."

When I got to her, Mellow was again flat on her side. There were some muddy streaks in the grass indicating that she'd been struggling to get up.

I picked her up and stood her back on all fours. Keeping my hands by her side, I waited to see how stable she was, ready to catch her. But, as soon as she had all four feet on the ground, she walked off as if nothing had happened. She was walking in the wrong direction, away from the barn, but she was walking.

With the help of my nudging and coaxing, Mellow finally arrived back in her hay bed. We were drenched, but she was safe once again. So I grabbed a towel and gently dried her off.

Mellow's physical ups and downs allowed me to closely observe not only her health, but also my actions. It was a conundrum: I wanted to do right by her and let her go when her time had come. But I also wanted to do right by her and keep her alive if she was still in good spirits. Ultimately, I decided I was ready and willing to provide her hospice care until the very end.

About a week later she came in from the field, limping more than usual. She could barely put weight on her right leg, and after watching her for forty-eight hours, John and I decided it was time to let Mellow go. Her quality of life seemed majorly compromised. We asked a friend to use his backhoe to dig the grave near Mellow's favorite grazing spot, and I made an appointment for the following day for Mellow to be euthanized.

The next day our vet joined us in the barn. After examining the Mellow, the vet told us that due to age-related osteoporosis, she appeared to have broken part of her femur-shoulder joint. It made her gimp but didn't seem to hurt. She was not dying because of it, and therefore it was still up to us to make the call if we wanted to let her go.

"Well, Doc," I said, "we had actually thought that you'd euthanize her today, but looking at her now, I'm not so sure."

Strangely enough, Mellow really didn't seem bothered enough by her injury to call it quits. Compared with the day before, she had a lot of energy. With the exam completed, she limped off to greet one of the vet techs. He was eating a jelly-filled donut. Mellow reached up, begging for a few crumbs. The tech gave her the rest of the donut, and Mellow was searching for more. I looked at the vet. "Yesterday I was sure she was ready to move on. She was lying in this aisle all day; she had no life energy."

We knew it was likely just a matter of days, but euthanizing Mellow as she was searching the vet tech's hands for the last speck of jelly seemed wrong.

After assuring me he was available to come on short notice "when the time has actually come," the vet and his crew headed back out.

John and I watched Mellow follow everybody out of the barn. She did a three-legged gimp over the barn doorsill and started yet another search for dandelions.

The next day I had appointments out of town. When I got home that night, Mellow was standing on all four legs. Miraculous!

The next three days Mellow was fairly stable, and I felt really good about having not rushed the ending. Watching her munching shrubs alongside the fence posts, I pondered the difficult choices we have to make when we're responsible for an animal. I constantly contemplated my options, wanting to do the right thing for Mellow while recognizing that her situation was not convenient. We could not leave the property for long without someone supervising her, and she would still occasionally fall over and need help getting up.

My goal was to see the situation through Mellow's eyes and put her needs before mine when determining what would be best for her. It was clear she was still enjoying life. She was a "tough old bird," rallying every morning to walk through the barn and into the sun, where she soaked up the rays. When I checked back in the afternoons, she was usually off grazing somewhere around the barn. Several times I tried to help her navigate, which she vehemently refused. It was bad enough she needed my help to get back on her feet; she definitely did not want me to help her across the sill of the barn door or around a fence corner. She seemed happy and glowing in the early-evening light.

Then came the day when Mellow fell over a lot. It was actually still more of a nuisance than cruelty to her. The moment she was up again, she marched on. But by the afternoon her spirit had changed. I could feel she was more frustrated and was losing strength. To prevent further damage, I confined her to her stall. We checked in on Mellow every hour to make sure she wasn't stranded on her side. Most of the time she was.

The next morning it was clear she was no longer able to stand on her own. I called the vet to tell him that the time for Mellow had come. Because she still had a strong desire to walk, I placed a towel under her belly to hold her up and walked with her through the barn. But for obvious reasons, that was not a feasible option for long.

While waiting for the vet, John and I placed two bales of hay on either side of Mellow to keep her upright. This made it possible for her to stand on her own while leaning on the bales. After many weeks of uncertainty it was suddenly clear. In her own way, at times subtly, at times not so subtly, Mellow had taught me to tune in so I undoubtedly knew when it was time to say our final goodbye.

PET LOGIC "PICK-ME-UP"

6.
The Benefit of Accepting Reality

"A Houdini she is" were the parting words from Rick, the farmer who had just sold us his little goat for fifty dollars. He had pointed to a variety of gates and fences, "Over this one, under this one, and through that one over there."

Once we got back into the truck, I looked at John, my husband. "A Houdini?" I said.

"Yes," John answered, "He said that the first time we came to check her out."

"I guess I didn't really listen," I mumbled. Half a mile down the hilly country road it started to sink in. What was I thinking? My intention had been good. I wanted to find a companion for Isaac, our aging sheep. We all were grieving the loss of Mellow, but no one felt it more than Isaac. For the last four weeks I had filled in as Isaac's companion as much as I could. But he wanted me 24/7, not understanding that I was also in relationships with nine other animals plus my husband.

In order to find a new companion for Isaac, I put out word that we were looking to rescue another goat or sheep, preferably a goat. Sheep have the tendency to baa loudly and constantly, and so I decided we were better off with another goat.

Through a neighbor, I learned that a farmer in the Hilltowns region had a young goat available who was ready to be weaned. The farmer wanted to feed the mom's milk to his family and was hoping to find a good home for the goat. He was also considering bringing her to auction. Needless to say, the word *auction* sprung me to action. Granted, the goat might have ended up in a dairy operation, not necessarily the meat market, but knowing the options I felt she was in need of rescue.

When John and I initially drove to the farm to meet the little goat, we thought she was adorable. She was shy, but also independent and, most important, healthy. The latter was John's requirement. Looking at the young goat, he said, "Would be nice to have a healthy animal for a change." He had a point. I have a soft spot for older animals with health issues, and the idea of having a young, fit animal to care for was enticing. We watched her climb over a rock formation in her paddock to reach a few hemlock branches, and we were sold.

Looking around the goat paddock, I noticed the mesh fencing. "We have a three-board rail fence for the horses," I said to Rick. "I take it that won't work for her?"

"Oh no, she'll need a mesh fence; otherwise she'll slip right through it," he answered.

"Hmm. How will we keep her from running all over the property, onto the street?" I asked. When neither Rick nor John answered, I continued, "Well, I guess we could fence in the area behind the garage. That's a nice shady spot where she and Isaac can spend their day."

On our way home, we stopped at the feed store to buy some goat food and two rolls of mesh fencing. That night a friend and I hammered the mesh to the fence posts to keep the goat and sheep from getting close to the road. By the time it got dark, there was only a small portion without mesh fence. I decided we could always fence that section in later.

The farmer's wife and daughter had called the goat Sandy because her overall color was white while the hair on top of her back looked dusted with a sand shaker. Sandy had not responded when we called her name during the first visit. So John and I opened ourselves to any signs suggesting a better name.

The day we were scheduled to get the goat, I woke up with the name Sammy in my mind. Though the name seemed similar, when I sounded it out, Sandy sounded hard and Sammy sounded so much softer. "I like it," John declared. "Sammy it is."

A few hours after the renaming, we headed to the farm, the three-horse trailer in tow. We had barricaded two of the stall compartments to create a smaller, safer space for Sammy's transport. When we arrived, Rick attached a lead rope to the turquoise collar Sammy wore around her neck and handed her over to me. She let me lead her onto the trailer without trouble. As I unhooked the lead rope, she started to call for the other goats, and I told her she was heading to her new home. Her energy shifted from curious to anxious. "You'll be okay, little girl," I said as I moved toward the exit, "It's a short ride." But before we were able to close the back door, Sammy had already gotten over and between the barricaded hay bales and was now walking around in the huge three-horse compartment right near the rear door. If I remember correctly, that was the moment Rick said, "A Houdini she is."

As soon as we got out of the driveway, John and I decided to review our plan one more time. The Houdini comment had us both worried. We would need to pull another fence line. John pointed out that the area I had chosen for the goat and sheep was open to the horse pasture. He looked at me. "If Sammy escapes into the horse pasture, she could run off to the road." He was right. In that moment I realized the original area I had picked also backed up to the barn, and its sloping roof was only two feet off the ground. "Considering what we just learned about our new goat," I said, "Sammy will be up on the roof in no time and probably fall to her death."

"In addition," John replied, "while you loaded Sammy, Rick told me that by the time she's all grown up, she will be able to clear four-foot-high fences. That two-foot gate you have in front of the barn to keep Isaac in is no obstacle for Sammy."

A million thoughts raced through my mind as I navigated the truck and trailer down the hilly country road. Sammy was nothing like the goat we had just lost. Mellow was old; she'd moved slowly. She couldn't jump over and around hay bales. This young goat was an entirely different story; I had just witnessed how fast she circumvented my hay-bale contraption. Next would be the roof and the gate.

At first I'd been excited about taking on a new family member. Now I realized that adding this young goat to our herd was more work than I had anticipated. "I think I made a big mistake," I whispered, eyeing the rearview mirror. "I think I need to turn this rig around and bring her back."

"What are you talking about?" John replied.

"I am overwhelmed that we are adding an animal that requires us to "escape-proof" the entire property."

Since it wasn't that easy to turn the big rig around on a narrow mountain road, I continued to drive. As scared as I was by the commitment I had made, I would also be embarrassed to show up at that farm again and hand Sammy over to Rick.

I'd thought it was going to be so simple: I would find a companion goat for the sheep so I could go back to working on my book without being sidetracked by Isaac standing at the back door baaing.

My mistake was to think that a goat is a goat is a goat. Mellow was well over ten when we got her. She was crippled and arthritic. She didn't jump over or crawl under fences. Sammy was barely a year old and full of piss and vinegar.

I could not ignore the irony: a year and a half earlier we had saved a goat and sheep from going to the auction. The goat eventually passed on, and the sheep got lonely. Now we were getting a new goat for the sheep we had never planned on having in the first place. Once the sheep died we would need to find another companion for the goat. The sheep-goat-sheep circle would never end, I thought as I continued on toward home.

Once we arrived at the farm, John and I went to work. We pounded metal fence posts into the ground, tied the mesh fence to it, and built makeshift gates. Sammy quietly waited in the trailer. I found that surprising, especially since she had just left her mom and aunt behind. I thought she would give at least a little *"meh"*... but she didn't.

Once the fence was erected, we opened the trailer and I clipped the lead rope on Sammy's little collar. She stood calmly in the opening and looked around. John suggested we give her a handful of grain. Good point. Let's make a good first impression. Rick had told us to feed Sammy some grain in the morning and at night, not because she needed grain but because it would associate positively with the barn and the new people.

Once she had a handful of grain, Sammy jumped off the trailer. John walked her into her new enclosure while I took some pictures. The pen was quite different from what she was used to. She had lived in a rocky, dry paddock; at our house she had grass and a few shrubs. The night before we had picked her up, I had done some research and learned that goats, much like deer, are browsers. They like to nibble on bushes and branches. Sheep, on the other hand are grazers, like cows and horses. Our old goat, Mellow, had been free to roam, and she usually hung by the edge of the pastures to nibble the branches. Our newly built pen wasn't ideal; it had more grass than shrubs, and therefore Sammy would have to be turned out on the grass in stages to prevent bloat, an accumulation of gas in the stomach that can be life-threatening. She would have to be in the new pen for an hour a day, then two, then three, to get her sensitive stomach used to it. This caused two issues: one, that I needed to keep an eye on the clock and move Sammy in and out of that pen on time; and two, I needed to figure out where she could stay—aside from her stall—for the rest of the day.

Somehow this whole ordeal turned out to be the exact opposite of what I had hoped for: my to-do list was growing by the minute, when I had hoped for things to become less complicated.

For a while, John and I hung out in the backyard with Sammy. We wanted her to bond a little with us before we brought Isaac out to join her, and she was definitely seeking our company. Every few bites she came up to us to get a pet or scratch before going back to exploring the grass and shrubs. At one point she got up on her hind legs to nibble the lower branches of a tree right next to the fence. Stretched up like this, she was tall, very tall. John and I looked at each other, and then eyed the fence. This was going to be trouble.

Once we brought Isaac into the pen, Sammy's interest was split between him and us. Isaac seemed mildly interested in Sammy's lively energy but after ten minutes he asked to be let out of the pen. He stood at the gate *baa*ing his little heart out. We convinced him to stick it out a little longer, but after thirty minutes he was done. And so was Sammy. She stood next to Isaac by the gate interspersing his "*baa*"s with her little "*meh*." On the one hand, we understood—Isaac was used to going wherever he wanted. On the other hand, John and I felt they needed to get used to their new setup and decided to go into the house to have lunch. When I went out an hour later, things had not improved. The moment Isaac saw me, he went to the gate and begged to be let out. He was tired and wanted to chill in the barn. The timing was right anyway; Sammy had had enough grass for the first day. Our barn was large enough; they could spend the afternoon roaming around in there before retiring to their stall later in the afternoon.

The moment we entered the barn, I realized it wasn't going to be that simple. Sammy was absolutely fascinated by the many things I had stored in there. She had to check it all out, and before I knew it, she had her nose in the bucket I had designated for odds and ends. She smelled the fly spray, chewed on the brushes, picked up the roll of paper towels, and reached for the hoof pick down near the bottom. Next she moved on to nibble the bristles of the broom leaning against the wall before she got on her hind end to reach the shelf that held shampoos and conditioners. I pulled her down with her collar to get her feet back on the ground, but the moment I let go, she marched over to a bridle hanging on a hook and started to chew on the reins. It became clear that I had to clean and reorganize the barn if I wanted this to be the space in which Sammy would hang out for the next six hours before bedtime. So I went to work.

The next day we repeated the routine. Grass in the morning and barn time in the afternoon. Sammy and Isaac seemed to be getting along great. There was no need for me to babysit them in the barn. Finally I was able to focus on a few other things on my original to-do list.

That night when I entered the barn to feed the animals their dinner, my breath caught in my chest. Sammy had "explored" whatever I had not put away properly the day before.

She had tipped over a lamp, broken a window pane, and cleared off the top of a high chest of drawers. On the floor I found glass shards, wooden garden ornaments, most of them broken, and a large jar of horse treats. The lid was off and only five little treats were left on the very bottom. Looking at their satisfied faces, I could see that Isaac and Sammy didn't need dinner.

After I locked them both into their stall I started the second barn cleanup. As I pushed the shop vacuum across the floor, I started bawling. I had a hard time accepting my reality. What the heck had I gotten myself into? What part of this was making life easier for me? No matter where I turned, the mess got messier.

Forty-five minutes later I finally headed back to the house. John was hanging out on the porch. "I can't do this!" I cried as I flopped onto the wicker sofa. "I really think I made a big mistake." Then I shared what I had just encountered in the barn. "The worst part is," I continued, "Sammy is perfect. She is a goat; that's what goats do. I just didn't realize what it meant to have a goat because Mellow was so *not* a goat. And Sammy is so sweet, I like her so much, but I don't think I can handle it."

John was concerned. It wasn't like me to be a blubbering, crying mess. He said, "Why don't you call her former owners and tell them that we've realized this is not working out. We just don't have the right setup for a young goat."

As enticing as his suggestion was, I wasn't sure I could do that. The family was glad they had found a home for Sammy. What if their response to my call was, "Okay, we'll pick her up on Tuesday and bring her to the auction"?

I wondered if I was trying hard enough to make it work. Though I felt beyond overwhelmed, I also wanted to be fair and mindful about Sammy's future. Could I live with her going to the auction? No! Could I try harder to make this work? I wasn't sure how.

One of my neighbors had a herd of goats, and I decided to call and ask her to pleeeeaaase come over to help me find a solution. My hope was she'd fall in love with Sammy and offer to take her.

The neighbor and her husband came the next morning. I had left Sammy in the barn, and though she won over the neighbors' hearts immediately, they did not offer to take her. The husband did point out what we had already realized: our pasture fence was not going to contain her, unless we were willing to wrap the entire twelve acres in mesh fence.

We weren't.

After walking around the barn and the adjacent meadows, the neighbor finally summed it up: "You have just got to let her be. She will get used to the horses, and she will stay near the barn. Goats really bond easily." We had to agree with that. "And you'll just have to trust that she's not going anywhere. She will eat your flowers, but aside from that, I wouldn't worry so much."

"I hope you're right," I said, still believing I would be better off if the neighbors took Sammy.

"Look at her." The neighbor pointed at Sammy. She had snuck through the gate and was now visiting with Jesse, our eighteen-hundred-pound draft horse.

Watching that little scene, John appeared to warm up to Sammy living with us. "You know, Nicole, maybe it's simpler than we think. Maybe we've just got to have the attitude that she needs to get used to her new home. She'll get used to the horses, learn about the fences, and will know the barn is her home. Hopefully she'll never run too far from it. Let's give it a try for two more days and see how it works out."

I was hesitant but willing.

After the neighbors headed out, we left Sammy and Isaac with the horses. When we checked up on them an hour later, they were grazing and browsing in one field, the horses in another. When Sammy saw us, she called out, "*Meh-he.*"

I responded, "What a good girl you are, hanging out with Isaac and the horses," figuring positive reinforcement might help here too. Walking back to the house, I took what seemed like the first breath in days. Maybe this *was* going to work out.

Ironically, the more I relaxed and accepted my new reality, the more barn-bound Sammy became. She never left Isaac's side for more than a few minutes, and when she was out of sight, she'd call out to let him know where she was. She also started to bond with our thirty-three-year-old horse, Jesse. After about a week I saw Sammy lying flat on her side, napping next to Jesse, who was watching over her.

Today Sammy is doing more of the same: she hangs with the herd in the fields and still crawls under the pasture fence to take a walk around the property. And yes, she eventually found access to the barn roof and has danced around on it a few times. However, she has also shown herself to be a wonderful healer. Her abundance of energy had initially been overwhelming for Isaac. But over time, it has rejuvenated him. He's still going strong at age twelve. And whenever a horse is not well and needs some companionship, she is always close by.

When both Sammy and Isaac are out and about on the property, they occasionally show up at the mudroom door, *baa*ing and *mehe*ing for me to come out and keep them company. I do whenever I have the time. But I don't feel guilty when I can't, because they now have each other.

Sammy has certainly shown me that an innocent idea can have unexpected consequences. The first thing I had to do was to accept the reality I had created. Once I did, the chaos left and peace on the farm, and in my mind, was restored.

PET LOGIC

"THAT'S THE SPOT"

7.
The Magical Red Sofa

As I was driving home from the local dog park with my yellow Lab, Amber, my eyes fell on a red sofa standing beside the road. On quick glance it looked exactly like the sofa I was hoping to find for my office. I pulled over to check it out more closely. Yes, it had the design I wanted, the size was perfect, and the color was just what I'd hoped for. And, it was adorned with a yellow sign: free. I had searched everywhere for this sofa: Craigslist, eBay, local antique stores, and not so local antique stores. This particular kind of sofa was not easy to find, and the ones I had found were very expensive and usually located in the most western part of Pennsylvania or in the antiques malls in San Antonio, Texas.

I turned into the driveway and got out.

Upon closer inspection I understood why the sofa was free. Cats had gotten the better of the fabric at each of the front corners. The stuffing was puffing out, and the wooden legs had a few scratches. I would get it reupholstered and restore the legs. It wasn't perfect, but it was perfect enough for me.

The challenge was to figure out how to get the sofa into my truck bed. The house seemed quiet; there was no one to give me a hand. As I was going through a list of friends I could call to come help me out, I noticed a woman and her dog walking alongside the road.

When she got closer, the woman immediately offered her help and tied her dog to the running board of my truck. Within moments the sofa was in the truck bed. As I closed the rear gate, she released the pup from the running board while I thanked her profusely.

Of course I couldn't resist petting the pup. Not wanting to assume, I asked what type of dog she was and the woman told me that Sadie was a pit bull. Turned out she and her husband had a foster home for pit bulls and Chihuahuas. "What an interesting mix," I said. "One might expect that the Chihuahuas are dinner for the pit bulls." The woman laughed and said that it was actually the opposite—the Chihuahuas were running the pack.

As I petted Sadie, the woman introduced herself as Chris and shared a little more about her dog. Eight years earlier Sadie had been a bait dog. She was kept in a basement in a building in a nearby town. People had cut her skin with knives until she bled and then sent a bunch of fighting dogs Sadie's way.

Helga, another rescue dog, was found in a basement as well, ripped to shreds, pregnant, and, as it turned out, suffering from stomach cancer. Chris and her husband took Helga to a veterinary specialist in Boston and spent five thousand dollars on surgery. Their daughter, a vet tech at a local rescue shelter, developed a holistic cancer-treatment plan following the surgery, which gave Helga another eight months of joyful life.

Because of Helga, Chris told me, the clinic now provides this particular holistic treatment to all dogs with similar cancer because it had proven to be a great supplement. Helga, once a helpless, abused, neglected pup, had become a catalyst for the betterment of other dogs.

Chris shared that she was happy to know that Helga had one year—her last—filled with joy and doggy fun. They had taken her to Maine, swum in a lake with her, and provided her with love she'd never known.

I could relate. I told Chris about my late horse Star. We had met when I was looking for a therapeutic riding horse. A volunteer had told me about Star, but when we went to check him out, I was horrified. Star lived in a small, fenced-in area of backyard. His enclosure housed a chicken coop, a bunch of metal trashcans, and a low-ceilinged ratty shed that was his shelter. Besides wanting to take him out of this unsuitable environment, I felt an immediate attraction to this little gray horse. But back then I did not have a barn. And he did not seem a good match for the riding center. Thankfully, a friend of mine adopted him.

A few years later I reconnected with Star and our connection was still flowing strong. He gave me many signs that he wanted to live with me. Every time I came for a riding lesson at his barn I'd visit with him, and each time he'd point his head toward my horse trailer as if to say, "Get me in and let's go." Eventually, during a meditation workshop, I tuned into Star and dared to ask him, "Do you want to live with me?" Before he could answer, I specified, "I promise you, you will never have to live like you did when we first met. However, I do not have green pastures like you have here."

He replied, "A true connection is more important than green pastures." That, of course, sealed the deal. Star lived with us for about a year before he got a chronic hoof disease called laminitis and eventually passed. Just like Helga the pit bull had taught Chris, Star during his last few months taught me about his illness and how to stay present during challenging times. Now Chris was in tears.

We spontaneously hugged and looked misty-eyed at that red sofa. Simultaneously we said, "That is some sofa."

"Yes," I said, "it is magical." How often do we get to connect in mindful ways with like-minded people on the side of a road?

PET LOGIC

"INDOOR/OUTDOOR CAT"

8.
The Wild is Calling

While I volunteered at a wildlife rehab center one day a boy and his mother dropped off a box containing seven bunnies. The boy had found the bunnies while playing in the backyard and thought they had been abandoned. Unfortunately, the family—like so many others, me included—didn't know much about wild rabbits. The director explained that the mother of the bunnies most likely had fed the youngsters early in the morning before she headed off to do what adult rabbits do: eat, play, and eat some more before eventually returning home to take care of their babies.

"At this point it's too late to put the bunnies back into their nest. We'll take care of them and try our best to keep them alive," she said. After the mother and son left, we gathered around the table looking at the seven little bunnies, eyes barely open, little ears still stuck to their heads, tucked into a box that once housed a pair of sneakers.

The director of the rescue explained that these youngsters were most likely not going to survive. Though she warned that bunnies are very sensitive and delicate, I still wanted to give them a chance. One of the volunteers took three of the babies, and I ended up with four. We were instructed to feed them twice a day with tiny little syringes while holding them wrapped in a little hand towel so they felt safe and protected. I took one of the small terrariums from the center and when I got home filled it with soft fabric and fleece hats so the little guys could burrow themselves.

After a week I reported back to the director that all the bunnies were still alive and hopping. She was amazed. The other volunteer had reported that unfortunately, her bunnies did not make it.

For the week following I introduced deep-green leaves of lettuce and paper-thin apple slices to the rabbits' diet. They loved them. A week and a half later they had grown to more than double their size and moved around much more. I felt they needed a larger enclosure and found a birdcage in the garage, perfect to start the transition to the outside. On sunny days I simply put the cage on the grass. Through the bottom wire, their little feet got used to the sensation of grass, and they were able to listen to the sounds of the environment: birds, traffic, footsteps, and bugs.

Another week went by, and I started the weaning process, only one formula meal a day and otherwise water and lots of greenery—grass and clover, lettuce, and an occasional apple slice. As the bunnies grew older, it became clear that they were wild. The director had instructed us not to treat them like pets; they needed to maintain their innate flight instinct in order to survive in the wild. Because they were not being tamed, the bunnies were harder and harder to catch as they raced around the cage. And it became challenging to keep a hold of them during the bottle feeding. By day sixteen I decided to stop the hand feeding. The director of the wildlife center had explained that the expression "scared to death" originated because rabbits could be literally scared to death when they couldn't escape. I was afraid the rabbits would eventually meet this fate because of my handling and everything we had accomplished would be for nothing.

I sensed that the wild was calling to them, and I was glad the release date was just around the corner. The director had suggested setting the rabbits free on day twenty-one.

The night of day eighteen I looked into the cage and my body froze; one bunny was stretched out lifeless in the right corner. The remaining three huddled on the left side.

I glanced around the cage. What could have happened? The food was gone, they had water, and nothing looked unusual. I wondered if this was the little guy who had always sat by himself, the one who ate slowly and usually hid under a pile of blankets. It crushed my heart to take him out of the cage. Though I knew I had done everything in my power to give these babies a chance, it was still devastating to lose one. After burying the bunny, I checked back on the other three. They seemed more anxious than usual, their movements more panicked. Occasionally they climbed up the side panels of the cage, only to be held back over and over again. I sensed urgency and wondered if I needed to release them right away. But it was late at night and pitch dark; I didn't want to act impulsively and risk their safety. So I decided to wait until morning.

When I woke up, I dreaded walking downstairs. What if all the bunnies had died? What if it was too late to release them this morning?

When I finally glanced into the cage, I saw that all three bunnies were breathing. They had calmed down considerably, however, I felt we were at a crossroads. The bunnies might have still been a few days too young to be released. They might not be able to survive on their own, but the alternative of keeping them was no guarantee for survival either. My responsibility, I decided, was to let nature take its course.

After feeding them another big meal of lettuce and apples, I took the cage into a grassy meadow that was far away from the road and surrounded by protective brush.

Then I opened the cage, and one, two, three, the bunnies stepped out and moved hesitantly off, each in a different direction. I left a head of lettuce and told them how grateful I was to have been able to care for them. Then I picked up the cage, turned back toward the house, and sent a safety prayer their way. In order to see the world from their point of view and respect their wild nature, I had to put my desire to protect them aside. I had given them a start; the rest was up to them.

PET LOGIC "WET DOG SMELL"

9.

The Perils of Harvesting Horsehair

The inside of the thank-you card to the participating practitioners read:

> *Jesse, our 34-year-old Percheron, is the inspiration behind the 1ˢᵗ Equine Wellness Expo.*
>
> *Through TLC and the efforts of several amazing holistic practitioners, Jesse has come back to health in body, mind, and soul. Witnessing his healing, I knew that more people needed to know about holistic equine wellness practices, and the Expo was born.*
>
> *Jesse and several other rescue horses have donated their hair for your gift, a horsehair key chain.*

This copy did not convey the conversations I'd had with Jesse since conjuring up the idea for the Equine Wellness Expo.

It had been four months since I'd received Jesse from the draft horse sanctuary, and in that time a small and talented team of equine wellness practitioners had contributed to his holistic healing. The changes in his health had been nothing short of miraculous. Through the love and compassion of strangers, he came back to the quality of life he so deserved.

If Jesse was able to recover, I knew other horses had a chance as well. People just needed to know about the treatments available, so I founded the Equine Wellness Expo, an event where holistic equine practitioners could showcase their skills to the local horse community. The funds raised would be given to the sanctuary Jesse had called home.

I wanted to thank the practitioners volunteering at the event with a small gift. I knew of a local woman who crafted jewelry out of horsehair and I placed an order for several handmade key chains, to show my appreciation.

Excited about my idea, I went to the barn to ask Jesse if he would donate some tail hair for this purpose. I explained that it was for the people who had helped him get better, as well as several others who were aiding the health of other horses in different ways. I waited for a response from him. I sensed he needed more explanation, and so I went on to describe my idea of the expo, where horse practitioners could show their skills in demonstrations and workshops while the local horse community could learn about the modalities available in the Pioneer Valley. It would be held at the Hadley Farm Equine Center at the University of Massachusetts. Even after I offered these additional details, I felt Jesse gave me, if anything, a shoulder shrug. He wasn't all that communicative in those early days, and I figured we'd revisit the idea when the time came.

Six weeks went by before it was time to collect some tail hair. I wanted to wash Jesse's tail before cutting it, so I concocted a yummy lunch that would keep him occupied while I got to work with a bucket of warm water and shampoo. Jesse munched quietly as I massaged his thick black hair, big white bubbles forming. For a moment I was led to believe that he actually enjoyed it.

But three quarters of the way through his meal he suddenly raised his head, took a deep breath, made a 180-degree turn on his hind end, and marched off. Sudsy tail swinging, he walked across the pasture, through a gate, past the hayloft, and through several more gates to finally stop on the opposite side of the property in front of the barn.

When I came around the other way to meet him in the barnyard, water bucket in hand, I could tell he was not happy. His eyes had gotten darker, his mood agitated. To get the suds out of his tail, we would have to start negotiations. Despite my very good arguments that walking around with a soap-bubbled tail was not healthy, and that his tail would start itching if we didn't get that stuff "outta there," when I tried to put on his halter he did not cooperate. After several attempts to slide the halter over his ears while he raised his head six feet and higher, I got my husband to put it on and hold the lead rope the best he could, while Jesse danced around, avoiding me and the water bucket. In fear of getting kicked, I finally grabbed the hose. I had to get this foam out of Jesse's tail—unfortunately now with cold water. That was not at all what I had planned, but it was better than leaving the shampoo in. Holding and hosing a reluctant, raging eighteen-hundred-pound horse was no treat for us. By the time we were done and Jesse released, we were exhausted and he stormed off in a huff.

That night, when I brought him his dinner, he still seemed a little reserved. The next morning after breakfast I waited for him in the barnyard where he would usually seek me out to get a little TLC. This morning was different.

He stood quietly near the fence, looking at me but not moving my way. Eventually I walked up to him and apologized for my intrusion the day before. I told him that I understood I had made a deal with him upon his arrival at our farm that he did not need to do anything he did not like to do. And obviously, as I had learned, washing his tail fell into that category. However, I went on to explain, I felt that it would be nice for him to provide some of the hair for the key chains. After all, he was the inspiration, and several of the practitioners had contributed to his well being.

He turned his head, looked at me, and gave me a piece of his mind. "Lady, I have served humans for over thirty years. Don't even think that any of the things you or any of the other people are doing right now will ever make up for what I have given of myself over the years."

That stopped me in my tracks. He had a point. As a young horse he started logging firewood, then moved on to become a carriage horse at a livery in New Haven, Connecticut, for twenty - some years. The last few years at the horse sanctuary he had still pulled couples in wedding carriages and kids on hayrides.

His statement made me apologize once more for my assumptive behavior, and I started to brush and stroke him with my hands while telling him that I had finally gotten the message and that I understood that he was here at his retirement farm to receive, not to give.

My hands ended up at his left front foot. Running my fingers along the top of the hoof, I found a piece of scab caught in a strand of hair. Since I couldn't pull it off, I stood up and told Jesse to wait a minute while I got a pair of scissors. When I came back I told him my sole intent was to remove the strand of hair that was tangled in the scab. As I snipped around on his ankle he suddenly moved two steps forward. I crawled back up to his front leg to continue, telling him to be patient for just another moment. The last thing I wanted was for him to get upset again.

But again he took two more steps. And I was once more required to crawl forward. The moment I was back in position next to his front leg, Jesse moved again. This time he took four steps, which put me right next to his left hind leg.

At that point I realized that he had moved forward with intention. Not for nothing was I now positioned right next to his tail. I stood up and looked at him, asking, "Are you telling me that I can take a little bit of your tail hair?" I felt a subtle sense of urgency from him. So I took a strand of his hair and snipped it off. Looking at him sheepishly, I asked, "One more?" His energy read: "Quick, now," so I snipped another strand. I sensed that I was allowed to take a third strand, and so I did. After that Jesse took a deep breath and walked away. There I stood with three strands from his tail after all. It wasn't enough for all the key chains, but it was an act of generosity. Some of the other horses at the sanctuary would give us the rest.

The day of the expo, the jewelry maker gave me the bag with the key chains. They were beautiful: black and white horsehair braided into unique and useful keepsakes.

"Sorry, Nicole," the woman said. "The package with Jesse's hair arrived too late, I did not get any of his hair into the key chains." I gulped. Did he and I go through all that tail washing craziness for nothing?

"However," she continued, "there is a gift in the bag for you, made of Jesse's hair."

I opened the little white box, and in it, curled into several circles, was a bracelet and a necklace made from beautiful black shiny horsehair. It was *my* perfect keepsake. Throughout the day, every time I looked at my wrist I felt connected to Jesse, my inspiration behind this special event.

PET LOGIC

"SEASONAL HELP"

10.
Ask and You Shall Receive

While visiting my parents who were vacationing in Florida, we decided to take a guided tour through the Everglades. I was amazed to learn about this incredible national park, the largest subtropical wilderness in the United States.

After seeing alligators and beautiful wild birds such as egrets, osprey, and ibis in their natural habitat, we visited an animal park that cared for "nuisance" alligators. An alligator earns this designation after being fed by humans. We learned that alligators enter gated communities through the extensive water channels that can be found throughout Florida. Once people in the communities have fed a gator, it becomes a nuisance when it crawls up the banks and wanders into backyards looking for food. At that point the authorities are called, and the alligator is brought to an animal park, where it stays contained for the rest of its life. It was sad to see these powerful animals stuck near a small water hole at a zoo, all because people had disregarded the signs that read: *Do not feed alligators, because the feeder becomes the food.*

Our last stop for the day was a reptile and bird sanctuary. We had barely entered the animal enclosure when a shriek caught my attention. Out of the corner of my eye I saw several large birdcages standing together. Someone from those cages clearly wanted to get the visitors' attention. Ignoring the shriek, our guide, the animal caretaker, walked us over to a terrarium containing baby alligators. Just as the guide took two alligator babies out of the tank, more shrieks echoed across the small building. This time the guide responded, bellowing, "Stop it right now, or you're gonna be in trouble."

When another high-pitched *"sreeeeeetch"* bounced off the metal walls and interrupted the baby-gator presentation, the caretaker, who had just handed the baby gators to my mom and another woman, picked up a spray bottle, stepped toward the cages, and called out again: "Just wait. You're gonna be in trouble."

This guy sounded serious. And that got me curious. Who was the screamer?

While the guide and the rest of the group moved on to meet a thirty-foot-long boa constrictor, I walked over to the birdcages, wondering who was asking for attention.

As I drew closer, the beautiful salmon-colored cockatoo in the first cage perked up. "*Sceeeeeeeeetch!*" he called out to me. Immediately I put my finger over my mouth and said, "Shhhhhhhhhhh, you're gonna be in trouble."

The bird responded by pushing a tiny "*pheeeeeb*" through his barely open beak. I couldn't believe it. Had this bird just listened to me?

His golden cage being the only thing between us, I asked, "Can you make another noise, something nicer?"

The bird replied with a melodic whistle, "*Fhlededede.*" This was perplexing. I got the impression this bird really understood me. Then, out of the blue, the cockatoo had another outburst. He sent out another shrill scream for all to hear.

Again I put my finger over my mouth to shush him, and he again offered me a quieter version of the same note. "Great, beautiful, can you make another sound?" I asked.

"*RAH RAH RAH RAH,*" he answered.

"All right, that is different," I said. "How about one more, but something really, really quiet?"

It was incredible. Suddenly the cockatoo sang, the little tongue vibrating: "*Dridriridridri.*"

"That is very nice, thank you," I replied.

By now my mother had come over to watch me. "Nicole, this is amazing."

"I know." I didn't take my eyes off the bird, "I wish I had this on video."

At that point I decided to change it up and asked the bird, "Can you do something with your feet?" The moment I said the words, he lifted his claw off the perch and pointed the bottom of his foot at me, basically giving me a high five.

My mom and I were cracking up.

"You are so cool. Please show me another part of your body," I said.

Now the cockatoo lifted his shoulders and bobbed them up and down, shrugging his wings. I laughed out loud. This bird was too much!

Intrigued by our little tête-à-tête, people had gathered around the cage. A woman to my left said, "If I didn't see it, I wouldn't believe it!"

"Can you show me one more thing?" I asked the bird, hoping I had not blown it with one too many requests. "What do you think?" The salmon-colored bird took a moment before he started to shuffle his little feet to the right. He shuffled until his body touched the cage, and when it did, he cocked his head to the left and pushed his little neck even closer into the cage wire. I took that as an invitation. "Do you want me to scratch your neck?" I asked. Since he didn't move away, I dared to stick my finger between the wires and worked my way into his feathery neck.

My experience with birds was very limited; I'd once pet a chicken, running my hand over her back. I certainly had never touched a bird down to skin level.

As my fingers explored, I noticed how the fluffy feathers turned into strong shafts the closer I got to the skin. And the skin itself was so soft and seemingly delicate. This was amazing and intriguing. Yet after a few strokes I pulled my finger back. I didn't want to overdo it and annoy the bird. I wanted to read his response to make sure he wanted more. "Did you like it? Do you want more?" I asked. The bird pushed his neck deeper into the wire, inviting me back. And I followed his wish. He had the fluffiest, feathery fur, deliciously soft, and he seemed rather smitten as he blinked along with every stroke.

I was hooked. I could have continued for hours but sensed that the woman to my left was really itching to scratch the bird too, so I pulled away from the cage. "Thank you for the great chat," I said to the bird, and moved on to visit with some of the other animals.

Before we left the sanctuary I stopped by the cockatoo cage to say goodbye. "Hey, handsome, I wish I had our earlier conversation on camera so I could take you home with me. What a video that would've been." My feathered buddy simply listened, and then I realized that some of the most incredible moments in life couldn't be captured in a picture or video; they simply need to be experienced in the moment.

PET LOGIC "BUCKETS OF LOVE"

11.
Melting Down the Barriers

"Have you met the latest addition to our practice, Nicole?" my vet asked, as I was about to leave his office. I had stopped by to pick up some herbs for Amber, my yellow Labrador.

"No," I answered. "What have you got?" It was always fun to see the newest addition. My vet and his wife had a soft spot for strays and unwanted animals, and each time I came to their office they had a new story to tell.

Dr. P. opened the door to the back room. "Meet Asteroid!" Moments later a tiny black cat tiptoed around the corner into the vestibule. "Oh my gosh," I said as the little kitten headed my way. "Can it get any cuter?" He was adorable—pitch black—and only about three months old. "How did you get him?" The kitten pushed his forehead into my shin over and over, encouraging me to reach down and pet him.

Dr. P. picked him up. "Wait till you hear this one." He explained that a couple of neighborhood kids had brought the kitten to his office the week before, after finding him covered in blood on the sidewalk next to an apartment building.

Despite the bleeding from the mouth and a small cut below his lip that quickly cleaned up, the little guy seemed to be in relatively good shape initially. Under closer examination, however, it became clear that the kitten's breathing was shallow. Based on that and where he had been found, Dr. P. concluded that his little body had experienced a high-impact concussion that caused some of the microscopic air sacs located in the lungs to burst.

Curious about the injuries, Dr. P. asked the kids to show him where they found the kitten. When he investigated the scene, he found a lone mosquito screen in the nearby bushes. It belonged to a window of an apartment on the sixth floor of the building. He determined that the kitty was most likely not hit by a car but had actually fallen out of the window high above. Dr. P. called the authorities to report the situation. When the firemen knocked and rang the doorbell of the apartment without any response, they eventually broke down the apartment door and entered. There they found another skinny kitten skittering around and a dog locked up in one of the closets. Dr. P. later learned that the tenants had abandoned the place a couple of weeks earlier, leaving behind the pets. Scratch marks on the window screen indicated that when the starvation became unbearable, the little black cat had pounced at the screen again and again until it gave. At that point kitty and screen both went flying out the sixth-floor window, crashing onto the sidewalk below.

"And that's why we gave him the name Asteroid," Dr. P. told me, wrapping up his story.

"That's some story," I told him. "I guess Asteroid is the Lassie of the cat world, saving the lives of the other kitten and the poor dog in the closet."

The vet agreed. "Yes, we found homes for the other two." He glanced at Asteroid "Are you looking for a cat?"

"Not really," I replied. We already had my barn cat, Cookie, and Amber, our yellow Labrador. She was more than leery about any other four-legged animals in the house. "He's super sweet," Dr. P. said. "Check it out." He picked Asteroid up, turned him on his back, cradled him in the crook of his arm, and petted his belly. Considering that Cookie didn't let me hold her right side up for more than a few seconds, I had to agree that this upside-down kitty was indeed sweet. I'd felt his gentle personality when he'd bumped his little head into my leg. But I was not looking to adopt another cat.

"As you know, Doc," I said, "Amber is getting older, and I really feel she would have a hard time with another animal in the house. Obviously this little guy is not old enough to be a barn cat, and quite frankly, I'm not sure Cookie is looking for a companion."

On the drive home it was hard to get Asteroid out of my mind. He had spurred a familiar feeling. Every so often I would meet an animal and simply know he or she had entered my life for a reason. Occasionally I'd decided against my feeling, but whenever I acted on the sensation and brought the animal into my life, I was rewarded with more knowledge, a deeper connection, and some significant life lesson.

When I told my husband about the encounter at the vet's office, his first reaction was that we couldn't bring another animal into the house. Amber was an unusually anxious dog, extremely attached to me and to her routines, and bringing a new animal into her environment seemed unfair. I heard him and in part I agreed. However, I had a gut feeling that was hard to deny. Asteroid had seemed not just sweet but also trusting, despite the starvation. I suspected he was gentle enough that Amber would be okay if we gave him a home.

Two days later I had John convinced to at least meet the kitten so he could see for himself. On our way to the feed store we stopped at the vet. It took no time for John to be convinced: this little guy was special. Taking advantage of the opportunity, I explained that Asteroid could live in the mudroom and laundry area until he was big enough to go outdoors. At that point, he could use the cat door and would be outside more than inside anyway. We would keep him away from Amber as much as possible, making sure she was adjusting to the changes.

On the drive home Asteroid was quiet as a mouse. And though he spent the first day in the mudroom area, it took less than forty-eight hours before he was running around the house, exploring underneath the sofa, the fireplace, and the space beneath the stairs. I had felt bad having him locked away from us.

Watching him race around the house, I was reminded of the German word *flitzen*, which translates into "flit around." Since the name Asteroid wasn't rolling off the tongue that easily, John and I agreed to call him Flitzer.

Just as John had predicted, Amber wasn't thrilled about the new family member. The first night, when Amber rested next to me on the sofa, Flitzer jumped up onto the edge of the cushion to sniff her face. Amber immediately turned to look at me, saying, "What are you going to do about *this*?" I wasn't sure what to do. Chase Flitzer off the sofa, even though he was just curious to meet her? Make

Amber suffer through the sniffing? Eventually I asked Amber to turn around and face me so I could keep the little explorer away from her face. Of course now, with Amber's face in my lap, Flitzer started to sniff her haunches, then her tail. Amber, without needing to look at what was tickling her behind, tucked in her tail, and when that didn't stop the irritation, she pulled her entire hind end tightly underneath her belly.

I met John's eyes. "I know, I know. I feel bad for her, too," I said. "She is so uncomfortable with Flitzer in her space. But we will work this out." Then I turned to Flitzer. "You are so sweet, wanting to get to know Amber, but she is not sure about it, so please give her a little space."

The next evening we went through the same routine, Amber faced away from me, Flitzer sniffed her face, I asked her to turn, and then, with Amber's face in my lap, Flitzer continued to investigate the back end of his new roommate. So I asked him again. "Flitzer, remember what I said yesterday? Please give Amber some space." Surprise, surprise, he took one more sniff and then lay down with his back pressed against Amber's leg. Her leg twitched once before she took a breath and let her head sink a little deeper into my thigh. Now I took a deep breath as well. That had worked better than I had expected. I wondered if Flitzer had understood me or if he had felt Amber's discomfort and backed off on his own. Maybe both. No matter what, we had a new routine, and it seemed to be working for all of us.

About a week later, as I was preparing dinner, Amber and Flitzer joined me in the kitchen. With one eye on the vegetables, I kept my other eye on Flitzer, making sure he wasn't bugging Amber. Whenever he approached her nose-to-nose, trying to sniff her, Amber raised her head so high, he couldn't reach her. That was a message he eventually understood. I was thrilled Amber was finding a way to deal with the kitty's presence. The instinct that should have been so natural for a dog—to chase the little kitty away—was not natural for Amber at all. Amber had a history.

Up until age three, Amber was raised in a breeding kennel, with no exposure to life outside. The behavior she displayed the day I picked her up was a foreboding of what was to come. Within the kennel Amber ran around, wagged her tail, and climbed the chain-link fence just like all the other dogs did. Yet, the moment I had placed the collar on her and started to lead her over the threshold of the kennel door, she froze, then quivered. Once I had coaxed her over to my truck, it became clear she was in no condition to jump in. So I lifted her up and placed her on the bench seat on the passenger side before settling into the driver seat to start the engine. As soon as Amber felt the rumbling of the truck through the seat, her quivering turned to trembling. By the time we were moving down the road, she was shaking out of control.

With one hand on the wheel and one on her neck, I tried to soothe her, telling her it would get better from here and that she would—finally—have a fun life. None of this seemed to matter; she was a nervous wreck.

After we arrived home we were faced with the next challenge—to climb a stair. At that time I lived in a second-floor apartment. Outside the front door was one cement step. When I asked Amber to step up, she simply looked at me. Her eyes clearly expressed that she had no clue what I was asking of her. She didn't even realize I *was* asking anything of her. It was evident in that moment that I had no choice but to carry this (thankfully) small yellow Labrador not only over the step but also up the staircase into my apartment.

I had a lot to learn. Amber's psychology was so different from that of any dog I had ever encountered and it took me some time to understand her behavior. Running into other dog people, I often found myself explaining why Amber did not play with other dogs (she didn't know how), why I lifted her into the truck (she had never learned to jump), why Amber never left my side (I was her safety). I constantly tried to experience the world through her eyes while considering her history, her personality, and her current circumstances.

By the time Flitzer entered our life Amber had changed a lot. She was more trusting and much more relaxed. But watching Flitzer step around her, I believed his puppy-like movements triggered her anxiety. It reminded her of the litters birthed by her kennel mates that had yipped and yapped and occasionally bitten her ankles.

Knowing this, I saw it as my responsibility to help Amber and Flitzer. Neither had chosen to be with me, or with each other, for that matter. That had been my doing. Now it was my duty to offer Amber safety and Flitzer some direction. The opportunity to guide Flitzer came quickly. Though Amber wasn't your typical tail wagger, she occasionally gave me a wag or two. Now, as she lay in the kitchen looking up at me, her tail thumped on the hardwood floor twice. That was all that was required for Flitzer to go on attack. He threw himself on the ground behind Amber, clawed her tail between his front paws, and began chewing. Promptly Amber scrambled up off the floor, dropped her head, and scuttled away into the hall. I stopped Flitzer from following her. I didn't want Amber to lose trust and faith in me for allowing these things to happen, but I also felt it would be good for her to be a little challenged so she could realize the world was safer than she thought.

Flitzer had become incredibly responsive in taking direction whenever I asked him to slow down or back off. In addition, he was very patient with Amber and this helped her overcome the emotional challenge of sharing space. Night after night on the sofa, Flitzer sat by her side looking at her, unfazed if she turned her head away from his stare. He waited it out until Amber would turn her head back, take a deep breath and once again let her head sink deeper into my lap. Only then did Flitzer relax as well.

As long as Flitzer wasn't touching Amber, I let him do his thing. I just sat and watched him applying his skills. More than once I said to John, "He is killin' her with kindness." Because Flitzer was waiting it out, Amber eventually realized nothing bad was going to happen. And she slowly dropped her guard.

After Flitzer had established himself as a no-nuisance companion, Amber was comfortable when he snuggled up to her belly or under her neck. In one of my favorite pictures Flitzer is lying near her head, one paw resting softly on Amber's forehead.

By the time Amber reached her mid-teens she had gotten senile and even more reliant on her routines. During that time Flitzer's presence provided her comfort. At night on the sofa, she would look for him and wait until he arrived before settling in. He became a companion she and I had come to trust.

Over the years it became clear that Flitzer was able to break down outdated belief systems in humans and animals alike. When my mother and father visited us from Germany a few months after Flitzer arrived, my mom was of the outspoken opinion that cats did not belong in her bed. Subsequently, she kept the door to the guest room closed day and night. In the wee hours of the morning, she didn't close the door fully while going across the hall to the bathroom and Flitzer made his move. Unbeknownst to my parents, Flitzer sneaked into their room. My mother reported later over breakfast that she had been woken by the most amazing "alarm clock." Flitzer had waited under their bed until my parents were back asleep. Then he jumped onto the covers and began licking my mother's eyebrows. Surprised by the sandpaper sensation and the quiet purr in her ear, she woke up and, she proudly shared, did not move until he was done.

She explained that Flitzer eventually curled up next to her leg to take a nap. Together they snoozed for a little longer before getting up for the day. According to my mom, this was an unexpected but very nice experience.

Turns out, Flitzer wasn't just my mom's alarm clock—he was her wake-up call and a reminder of the gentle caring and the good company our pets offer us. Not only does she look forward to seeing him when she visits, nowadays she is disappointed whenever he doesn't show up in her bed.

Flitzer's latest project is Mimi, an older black cat who joined our family more recently. As gentle as Mimi is with humans, she is also possessive and extremely territorial. When other cats enter whatever she defines as "her" space, she gets defensive. The space under the dining room table is guarded through hisses, and the bed is secured as her domain through growls.

Employing the knowledge and wisdom I had learned from my animals with Mimi, I was conscientious about looking at things through her eyes and I supported her when she felt cornered. I also requested better behavior when she took her actions too far. Yet at times I felt I was stuck in a perpetual cycle of setting boundaries with a spray bottle while using essential oils to calm Mimi's nerves. Progress was slow, until once again Flitzer stepped in.

As so often was the case, Mimi had taken up residence on the bottom right of my bed. When Flitzer jumped onto the bed from the left, Mimi became immediately defensive. She assumed a fighting position, crouched low, spitting and sneering, ready to jump Flitzer. I froze. With no water spray bottle in reach, I knew this was a major cat fight in the making.

Except it wasn't.

Flitzer didn't move a muscle or a whisker. He simply stared at Mimi, and then stared some more. His calm breathing made me take a deep breath. I got the sense I was going to witness yet another Flitzer teaching moment.

Fifteen seconds went by, and Mimi's high-pitched snarl changed to a growl.

Flitzer, unfazed by the variation, looked on.

A few breaths later Mimi slooooowly lowered herself down into the mattress, softening her growl.

Flitzer didn't flinch, he just kept on staring.

More time went by before Mimi finally lay down on her side, stomach exposed, every so often expelling a little "*tzssss … tzssss …*"

Flitzer, who had initially sat on his hind end, now lowered himself to sit over all fours.

They stayed like that for a while. Then Mimi started to lick her paw.

This was amazing.

Once Mimi had expressed clear signs of surrender by showing Flitzer her belly, Flitzer had dropped his body into a nonthreatening position as well. Now she was cleaning herself, showing him how relaxed she had become.

Once the paw was clean, Mimi turned over and went to sleep.

At that point Flitzer closed his eyes, and I sat in awe.

Witnessing the communication between these cats, I realized how little it took for Flitzer to convey his point. Less was more and patience won again. He knew exactly what was required to melt the guard of the most obstinate roommate yet.

I am so glad I followed the hunch to bring little Asteroid into our home. My instinct was right: he was my teacher. Flitzer's ability to accept other beings, mixed with his Zen-like perseverance, transforms lives, mine included, and makes him definitely the Lassie of the cat world.

PET LOGIC

"GREENER PASTURES"

12.
Making A Mindful Decision

"What about this one?" David pointed to a friendly, but reserved looking dog on the webpage open on my laptop. Taking a quick look at the description I answered, "Definitely could be a match. She'd be worth meeting."

A few years back, after John and I decided to go our separate ways, I'd had to also say goodbye to Amber, my sweet Labrador. I was with her through her last breath as she transitioned from life to death and I missed her beautiful spirit every day. I needed to grieve and to get my life in order before adding a new family member. Now two years later, I was settled in a new relationship and ready for a dog. My partner David and I had three cats, three horses and a goat. Though horses are prey animals and cats are predators, I always found cats and horses to be similar in personality. While a dog stays at your side, horses and cats often keep a sense of independence. I couldn't wait to once again feel the enthusiastic companionship. I missed the way a dog could jump into the truck with me—all wags and wonder about where we might be headed, and come bouncing into the house for dinner and then be ready to snuggle by the fire.

When I looked further into this sad-eyed puppy on the computer screen, I saw that Casey fit all of our criteria for what we could handle in a dog. She was approved for households with cats, had a sweet nature, and was working hard on housebreaking. She'd been left too long in a crate that was too small for her body, so initially her feet were splayed, her elbows bowed and she was sway-backed, but in her foster home with nutrition and lots of exercises, she was now thriving.

In the end we picked two dogs that fit our profile: Casey and Glitter. Glitter was smaller, already two-and-a-half years old and her adorable face stuck out as much as her name. As luck had it, both dogs were offered through the same agency and the next adoption clinic was the following day. By 11:30 am we were on the road to upstate New York.

The first dog right at the entrance of the 'meet and greet' room was … Glitter. A volunteer held her leash as she happily bounced around, saying a quick hello by taking a one-second sniff and allowing a three-second pet. David didn't have a chance to greet Glitter because she was off looking at the next person.

The volunteer brought Glitter's attention back to us by offering a few treats. This time Glitter hung out with us for about seven seconds, but then a big black Labrador walked in and caught her attention.

One of the volunteers suggested I could sit on the floor and ask Glitter to join me. Within seconds Glitter was on my lap, and a few seconds later she was off it again. I tried to entice her a few more times, but she didn't stick around. Glitter was clearly overwhelmed by the six other dogs and volunteers, and the puppies in crates in the center of the room. And let's not forget the energy of the stream of people coming and going, all hoping to find 'the one.' As I looked across the room I noticed four of the other adult dogs were lying on their blankets; two were standing up observing the scene. None of them were bouncing around like Glitter. As my eyes focused one of the dogs, I realized it was Casey. I turned to David and said, "Let's go meet Casey."

There she was, lying on a blanket chewing on a big bone. After greeting the foster parents I kneeled down. "Hi Casey, sweet girl, what are you doing?" Casey stopped chewing her bone right away, sniffed me, and then appeared comfortable when I started to pet her.

Her foster mom told us Casey had been with her for only six days. She'd never had an accident in her crate, knew not to touch the birdcage and was generally sweet and well behaved.

I asked to walk her so I could get an impression of how much the initial neglect had affected her growth and conformation. There was the slightest hesitation when she got up but once on all fours, she seemed fine. Her back was long and hollowed a little behind her shoulders, and her left stifle joint was slightly outward directed, but she was already outgrowing her initial limitations. Being only eight months old, she had a good chance of overcoming it all.

She took a few steps toward the puppies in the center of the room, but when her foster mom asked her to come back, she turned around and lay back down on her blanket. David started petting her neck and when I saw she liked it, I scratched her back toward the butt. Within moments Casey turned onto her side and showed us her belly. We of course gushed and petted her some more. "She hasn't done this for us yet," the foster dad said and seemed disappointed.

David and I exchanged looks; this was definitely a great sign.

When we took Casey outside to see how she would do on the leash, she paid little attention to the hustle and bustle in the room and walked nicely alongside her foster mom, who said she hadn't done this when she first came in but after working on it for a day, she'd picked it up right away.

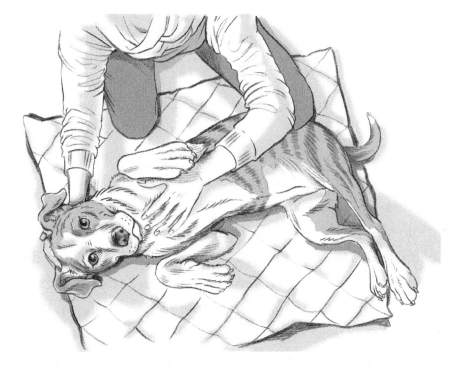

When Casey went to the bathroom on the lawn, the foster mom ran across the parking lot to get a plastic bag from a dispenser, and that was the only time Casey pulled, wanting to follow her. "Amazing," I said to David "She is already so attached."

Before we left, we stopped to visit Glitter one more time and though she was as cute as ever, she bounced from me to David back to the volunteer and then off to the next person, always at the end of her leash. I loved her little face, her size, her gender, but I also knew she'd be too much for the cats, and a lot for the horses and the goat to handle. And I wasn't sure if I could handle her. As a writer, I needed a certain amount of quiet time and it would probably be hard to get any with Glitter in the house.

"Just sit with it," the volunteer told me when I was having a hard time making a decision. "It has to feel right." And the moment she said it, I was suddenly clear: Casey felt right. I looked across the room at a family visiting with her. The parents were talking with the foster mom while Casey sat nicely in front of a little girl. She was calm and despite being only eight months old, incredibly well mannered. She was a mutt as many rescue dogs are, but I recognized a healthy dose of pit bull in her. I imagined myself taking Casey to events and talks and having her with me when I facilitated workshops and retreats for children at my farm. She seemed like a perfect match for our family.

On our drive back, David and I rehashed our experience and our feelings, and by the time we got home we were clear: Casey was the one. As soon as I could, I sent an email to the adoption volunteer telling her we had made our decision. We scheduled a home visit with a local volunteer of the dog rescue and were impressed by the thoroughness the rescue used in placing their pups. Without a doubt, their goal was to find a safe forever home.

Our home was approved on Thursday and Saturday at noon we heard from the foster mom that we could come pick Casey up. Within an hour we were on the road to Albany again to get our girl.

When we entered the foster home Cruiser, a dog the foster home had adopted a year earlier, and Casey came to greet us. Cruiser was a whirlwind, wanting to be petted, played with, and always looking to be the center of attention. And Casey was never far behind. The foster mom reported that Casey had gotten much more engaged in dog play over the last week and now held her own, so her hind end had gotten even stronger.

As if to show this off, both dogs played tug-of-war with an empty gallon water jug, and eventually rolled around on the floor in one big ball of goofiness.

After signing the adoption papers, I received the information pamphlet, Casey's collar, leash and blanket, and then we made our way over to the truck. Initially, we put Casey in the back seat, but when she became a little too curious about the crumbs on the floor, the seatbelts and the seat covers, we pulled her onto the front bench seat were she eventually fell asleep with her head on David's lap.

Occasionally I looked over and couldn't believe how happy I was to have a dog in the truck with me. I dreamed of our days on the road when we would teach people about creating mindful connections with animals, and Casey would become the ambassador of the often-misunderstood pit bulls.

Once we were home, she encountered our first feline family member ... Flitzer. Before I knew it, Casey was heading Flitzer's way while Flitzer stayed in place, his eyes growing to the size of saucers. I grabbed the leash tighter to pull Casey back and Flitzer puffed up, hissed and raised one paw, whacking at the air between them. Casey didn't think anything of it and kept pulling towards him, wanting to say hello. At that point Flitzer split and ran deeper into the house. Casey loved this sudden movement and her play-chase drive was now activated. She tried to go after him but didn't get far since I was white knuckling the leash.

That didn't go as planned.

Though we had hoped for a calmer introduction between cats and dog, we still went ahead with our plan to integrate the animals slowly by dividing the house into zones so the cats had access to the front half and the attic, while the backside of the house would be Casey's to roam.

This worked until the moment the cats wanted to go outside. They were used to going in and out at their leisure, and as expected, Sicily, the black and white cat, eventually showed up at one of the glass doors, telling us she needed to go out. Knowing Casey was a little too curious about the cats, David held her by the collar, while I brought Sicily into the mudroom. Then I closed off the mudroom area so the kitties could come back into the house, but not into the living space.

A while later, Flitzer tapped on the mudroom door to get back into the house. Again, David held Casey while I opened the door so Flitzer could stroll back through. This little ordeal went on and on, and though shuffling the animals around was pretty inconvenient, we were willing to comply if it would make for a good transition.

On day two Mimi, the cat with the most dog experience snuck into the kitchen and hopped on a chair that was pushed in under the table. When Casey made her way over to investigate, David suggested we see if they would work it out. Mimi is David's cat and she has a lot of sass and could possibly - with one quick hiss and swipe - teach Casey that cats are to be left alone. For quite a while Mimi held her own with Casey, she hissed, showed her claws, growled and bared her teeth. But the longer Mimi resisted playing, the more encouraging Casey got. She play-bowed, she barked and then barked louder. Eventually Mimi, just like Flitzer, ran and Casey ran after her. And that's when we learned that Casey didn't listen to her name, at least not when in chase mode.

Over the next couple of days all three cats showed us that this new family member was not welcome. On day three, Flitzer came with me when I went to feed the horses and started, out of the blue, spraying the grasses around the house. I had never seen him do this before. He was usually the one that integrated any new animals into our family circle. But Casey was just not listening to him and his subtle cues, and he needed to mark his territory.

Day four David sat in the kitchen and I in the living room when Sicily appeared at the glass door of the office once again. Casey ran over and with her nose on the glass and her tail wagging, she lowered her front-end to the ground. We were hopeful; maybe with this barrier between them, they could see and smell each other in a safe environment. But Sicily took a running start and with a howl threw herself against the glass door. To our amazement, Casey simply wagged harder.

Throughout the days we made mental lists of what we needed to work on. Even when distracted, Casey had to learn to listen to her name and to follow the basic commands of sit, down, leave it, and stay. We hoped reaching these goals would eliminate the chewing of the coffee table, the nibbling on the power cords and the paws on the kitchen counter.

Occasionally we used the crate, but since she had lived in one for so long, and loved her freedom, we only did that when we were feeding the horses or cooking dinner.

Part of our challenge was figuring out what it would take to tire out Casey. Two walks a day with tug-of-war in between was definitely not enough. Playing fetch in the backyard interested her only for a few throws at the most, occasionally I wrestled a little with her, but quickly realized though she was fairly gentle, she was no longer a puppy and her baby teeth had turned into sharp spikes. One day we took her to a big field where we let her off the leash, expecting she would run and release some energy. But no matter how hard we tried, Casey would not leave our sides. When I threw a stick for her she fetched it once and then lay down and started to chew on it. Luckily that day, there were no people around.

Out in public her worship for people had turned out to be challenging. Once out of the car, Casey usually sat beautifully, as directed, before crossing the street. But if there were people around all bets were off. One day, entering a mostly empty park, Casey saw a couple of maintenance workers picking up fallen branches. Without a warning she dragged me toward them. One of them called out "Can we say hi?" and before I could answer, Casey had already arrived at the guy's feet and was rolling around on her back while trying to lick his shoes.

When I gently tried to move her on, she dug in her heels and then tried to pick up a big branch nearby and drag it toward the maintenance truck. Enamored, she was ready to work for these guys.

Making her leave and come with me was challenging because our roles had reversed, now she was the one dragging behind me, as I tugged and pulled and tempted her with treats, trying to get her mind off those men. This whole scene was as concerning as it was endearing. It was clear that it would take a lot of work to get Casey's attention when she was as excited and distracted. I could enroll her in an agility or fly-ball class, but I couldn't imagine how we were going to incorporate in-depth dog training and weekend competitions across New England into our schedule.

One morning, when we realized our time with the cats had become almost non-existent, we decided to use the crate again. After Casey's morning walk, I put her back in her crate so we could snuggle with the cats. When Mimi entered the room she took one look at the puppy in the crate and her loud 'MEEOW' stopped me in my tracks. I looked down and suddenly she did something she had never done, she put her paw out and slapped my leg. I understood what she was telling me: I'd brought the unwelcome dog back into a room that was once her sanctuary.

Later that afternoon, Casey and I went out into the backyard. I threw the ball for her a few times and called out "good girl" whenever she brought it back to me. Hearing my voice echo across the yard and pastures, our three horses came trotting out of the field, looking for me. The horses had met Casey once before through the fence. Their responses were varied, Kaylaa, the older Arabian mare had stayed away; she was not interested in meeting the dog. Cutter, the Palomino quarter horse, had come to the fence to go nose-to-nose with Casey, but got quickly annoyed by the puppy licks around his nostril. Shana my younger Arabian mare, generally good with dogs, appeared irritated when Casey invaded her space, she lowered her head, pushed her nose toward Casey trying to get her out of her face. It was important to me that Shana got along with our new dog. She and I spend a lot of time together, and it was vital that Shana accept the dog as part of our life.

This afternoon, Cutter and Kaylaa had stopped at the far corner of the back yard. Shana however continued on and was now trotting alongside the fence. Casey, excited by her movement, decided to follow. Shana didn't change her speed, but the moment Casey caught up with her, her attitude changed. She turned a sharp right toward the fence, clearly indicating for Casey to back away. Instead Casey put her front paws on the fence, hoping to connect face-to-face with Shana. Shana, realizing she had to up the ante to bring her point across, did a swift 180 degree turn and threw a kick toward the fence. She never made contact but clearly expressed that she expected more respect.

When I looked down at Casey, I realized she was not fazed by it at all. She hadn't read the horse's energy, and I knew that without that critical intuitive skill, it would be impossible for her to ever fit in with the herd of our family.

And that was literally the final kicker.

After consulting with the rescue staff, it became clear that Casey needed things we could never offer: first and foremost another dog to help exhaust her puppy energy. Only then she would be able to learn new commands and change her behaviors. Clearly, no matter how much tug-of-war I played with Casey and how many miles we walked each day, I was never going to compete with the strength and endurance of another dog.

David and I decided it was time to explore our options, and we pulled out the Mindful Connections Wheel. After spending decades observing, documenting and analyzing the connections I've made with animals, this is the go-to tool I use when I have to make tough decisions or I am going through any kind of inquiry or crisis. The Wheel embodies the breadth of wisdom the animals have passed on to me, and helps me move forward when I am questioning the next step.

One of the five principals of the wheel is to see the situation through other's eyes. When we did this, it was very clear: the cats weren't happy, the horses weren't accepting, the humans were exhausted, and Casey was restless without a buddy.

Then we looked at our own life, and we couldn't visualize how we would consistently offer the attention and supervision Casey needed without neglecting our work and everyone else. One of the main tenets of the wheel is very simple: accept reality. We had to give Casey back.

The next day I sent an email to the adoption coordinator, letter her know our decision. One of the volunteers followed up with a phone call to learn what had and hadn't worked so she could pass it along, and then asked if we could keep Casey until Saturday when her former foster family was able to receive her again. We agreed to shuffle the kitties around for another thirty-six hours and decided to dedicate ourselves to Casey more than ever for the next day and a half soaking in every moment. Casey slept in our bed, went for a long walk in the morning, and then she and I visited a friend of mine where she got to play on the screened-in porch and lick a few more horses.

When we got home and Casey was still restless, we wrestled around in the backyard until I was tired and ready for a nap. Hoping for a few minutes of rest, I intuited a few therapeutic oils for Casey and offered them to her. Within minutes she joined me on the couch, her body splayed across mine for a snooze.

That last night she slept with us again, and when we woke in the morning we snuggled and played until it was time to go.

Of course, I was torn until the end. Casey was not only sweet and willing when not distracted, she'd also learned so much in our week together, showing she had the ability to grow and evolve mentally. Yet, when, on our way to the car, she nearly pulled me off my feet as she encountered Sicily in the driveway, I was reminded again why driving to Albany was a good idea.

As we waited in the parking lot for the foster mom to arrive, we told Casey how much she had taught us, and how grateful we were to have spent a week together. I mentioned that soon she would be reunited with her buddy Cruiser, which would make life so much fun again.

When the foster mom arrived my heart dropped. It was time to say goodbye, but before I could hug her Casey was already trying to get out of the car. As expected, she dragged me over to meet the new people, to say hello. It took her only a split second to recognize that this was not just any person, but the foster mom she had left behind. At that point she dropped her front end, threw herself into the foster mom's legs, rubbed her neck on her boots and wiggled her butt just like she had done with the guy in the park.

It was then, seeing Casey so happy and excited, that the guilt and sadness that had been hounding me began to melt away.

When we came home we cleaned the house, vacuumed the milk-bone bits, picked up baling twine shreds, gathered the toys we'd never used to bring back to the pet store, and put the raw hide treats we forgot to give to the foster mom near the door for our neighbor.

Then David and I sat down and took a deep breath. Moments later, the cats showed up.

There we were on the sofa, one cat to the left, one to the right, the third kitty on the sofa across the room. And in the quiet aftermath, I knew that heart-wrenching decision had been the right one, for everyone.

PET LOGIC

"GIFTS"

13.
Tenets of the Herd

Following the death of Okie, my handsome bay quarter horse cross, Cutter, our palomino, became the new herd leader. A few weeks into the loss, I helped out a friend and boarded her horse for a couple of months. At night I stalled the new horse in Okie's former stall and during the day put him in a separate pasture.

Daytime hours at our farm soon became horror hours. Cutter relentlessly ran down the fence line to charge the new horse. It was hard to believe that our kind and playful horse had turned into such a monster.

An obvious remedy for the situation was to move the new horse a few pastures or paddocks down and away from Cutter. Out of sight, out of mind. But that tactic would not give me any insights into why Cutter had changed.

Considering that Cutter and the rest of the herd were still getting used to life without Okie, I decided to bring Cutter into the barn, so he could hang with me while I mucked the stalls. I wanted to tune in to him and see if he would provide any clues as to how he was feeling. As I talked to him about his loss and his new role as herd leader, I noticed that he had parked himself right outside of Okie's stall.

A light bulb went on in my head. I asked him, "Do you want to move into Okie's stall? Is that the stall of the herd leader?" Cutter took a deep breath and blew out through his nose. He seemed relieved that I had noticed.

That night I switched stalls, placing Cutter in Okie's former stall and the new horse in Cutter's.

The next morning I let our horses out first and again brought the boarder to the adjacent pasture. Cutter took one look at the other horse, checked in with his mares, and then continued to graze. Later that day he met the new horse across the fence and established his leadership with a quick squeal followed by a nipping motion.

The next day was equally uneventful.

A week later the new horse joined the other horses and became a member of Cutter's herd. By acknowledging to Cutter that this stall was that of the herd leader, I had restored peace. Once again, I was the student and the horse the master teacher.

PET LOGIC

"TAKE A BREAK"

14.
Coming Home

I was not looking for a puppy, I truly wasn't.

We had barely recovered from the adoption of Casey that had turned one week of our lives into mayhem. Even though David and I knew we'd done the right thing by returning the Casey to the rescue agency, we still felt sorry and defeated.

Since we were about to pack up and move to a new state, we decided to put dog ownership on the back burner.

A couple of months later my friend Kate, a foster mom for a dog rescue, emailed me about a pup she'd fallen in love with at an adoption event. When I went online to check out her love interest, my eyes fell on another little dog named Dusty. His profile said he was an Australian Shepherd/Collie who had been abandoned in a field with his three siblings. What struck me most was Dusty's coloring; his body was snowy white with a single patch of chestnut brown over one eye. I emailed the picture of little Dusty to Kate saying, "This boy is about as cute as they get." She agreed.

Later she emailed back and told me that Dusty was coming up from the South, as many rescue dogs do, within the week and she and her daughter had decided to foster him. I felt a tinge of panic. I didn't want a puppy! Our experience with Casey had made me question whether I was even cut out to be a dog mom again. I was really good with horses, goats, and cats. Caring for a puppy... I wasn't so sure anymore. Plus we were just about to move and we'd need a dog that our animal family would approve of and embrace.

But Kate assured me there was no pressure. She thought Dusty was cute. She and her daughter would have a good time fostering him until he found his forever home.

I received the first email within hours of Dusty being with Kate. "Oh Nicole, he's so precious," she wrote, "He gets along great with our cat, he just sniffed with her nose-to-nose and then turned away. And he is great with our Labrador Rosie!"

A couple of hours later I got the second email. "What a sweetie he is," wrote Kate. "While my daughter is sitting on the sofa, Dusty is lying by her feet, stretched against her leg, napping. He doesn't jump on the furniture at all."

The next morning another email from Kate waited in my inbox: "Nicole, he's really wonderful. Dusty wants to be with us, follows us around. He is a bit timid about things that come from above, hands, shopping bags, etc. I will send some pictures tomorrow."

The following day I was so busy packing boxes and organizing the move that it was dinner time before I realized I hadn't gotten any news about Dusty all day. I sent Kate an email, sheepishly admitting that I'd missed her updates. My email crossed with hers in which she reported Dusty had developed swelling around his elbow joint and had been treated by a veterinarian, where he was staying for the night. She said Dusty wasn't accepting the crate training, had barked all night, and disturbed her neighbors. That meant Kate had to pass Dusty on to a different foster home once he was released from the vet.

And that's when I started to worry. At Kate's house Dusty was treated like a family member. She was observing him closely so she could provide me with the information I needed to make a wise decision. With him moving into a new foster home, the reports would stop, a new situation would be pressed on him, and the risk of him picking up some non-negotiable habits—like Casey did—was big.

Suddenly we were five days away from heading to our new home, and the puppy was on the move again as well.

Later that day, Caitlin, the adoption agent, emailed me "… it seems as if the timing isn't quite right. I'm thinking maybe it might be better to see what dogs we have available after you have settled into your new home. We have received a few applications for him and we need to be as timely as possible to ensure we get Dusty to his forever home as quickly as possible."

That email pushed me to action. I wrote back, telling her we'd spent the whole day in Vermont, getting the house ready so we could move sooner and have Dusty quicker. I described the farm—the 17 rural acres where we would all live—the horses, goats, cat, and now, our puppy. We told her we would be with him 24/7.

After I clicked send I sat still for a moment. Was this the right decision? Was I just reacting because there were other suitors? Was this truly 'our' dog and I shouldn't let him get away? I couldn't get a clear answer from my body, my mind, or my intuition. Everything was a scramble.

And then I remembered the time I'd turned down a snazzy little brown and white roping horse, a quick fiery ride. I walked away from this very affordable horse because I couldn't figure out where to keep him; but in reality, since I was living in Kentucky I could have probably placed him in a pasture at a friend's house. I never forgot that horse.

Was I willing to forget about this puppy?

Was I sure I wouldn't regret it?

I wasn't.

Luckily Caitlin wrote back quickly saying she was happy I would be able to adopt Dusty right away and asked me to send a video of our place in Vermont so she could get a feel for Dusty's new home.

I got the sense from what she said, that Dusty's next foster home was less a family and more of a large kennel that provided shelter, food, and some playgroups.

We sent the video that night and left the next day to visit Dusty at the kennel. On our way into Boston, Caitlin called and conducted her adoptee interview with me. She asked what drew me to Dusty, what our daily life looked like, how we would contain him on the property, and if we were willing to take him to dog training classes to make sure he got a good education. I elaborated that Dusty would accompany us during our daily animal chores, that we would be willing to fence an area if needed, but we hoped he could run free on our secluded lot. Our goal was to educate Dusty so he could become an ambassador for our mindful lifestyle, and go on the road with us to teach people about the wisdom of animals and the important roles they play in our human lives. If that meant hiring a dog trainer, we would be sure to find one.

Caitlin seemed satisfied and said that if we felt Dusty was right for us, I could fax the adoption papers to her, pay the fee online, and take Dusty home today instead of having to drive back into town a second time.

According to my GPS, we were getting close. And then my eye fell on a dilapidated building, and I was just short of saying to David, "Oh my God, what if that's the building?" when I realized, it *was* the building, an old warehouse, surrounded by a six-foot, chain-link fence.

As soon as we opened the door, the smell gave it away; a lot of dogs had lived and pooped there. Though the floor and the general vicinity were clean, it seemed more like a halfway house than a home.

A volunteer was waiting for us behind the large counter, and asked another girl to bring Dusty out. David and I sat on the leather sofa overlooking two empty playpens. Both had chest high plastic room dividers around the circumference, topped with Plexiglas.

Moments later the woman returned with Dusty at the helm. He came around the corner, took a look at us, and headed our way. I called out, "Hi sweet boy!" Which made him walk faster and a split second later the woman let go of the leash and Dusty's front paws were on my knees and he started to lick my hands.

"Hi baby boy, what a cutie face you are" I called to him while he raised his nose to my face and started to lick my chin and cheek. Aware of David's voice cooing similar words, Dusty turned to David and went through the same process again. He gave us lots of kisses on the hands and face and then he dropped back to the floor, looked at me and started walking toward the exit. I got up and followed. Dusty walked straight to the door, stopped and looked at me, saying, "What are you waiting for?"

"He thinks this is a done deal," I told David. I faced the pup and said, "Let's go back and talk this through."

Back on the sofa I whispered to David, "What do you think? Are we ready to make a commitment after knowing him for three minutes?" We started laughing.

"He's certainly cute, and seems to be a good boy," David said. I agreed, but didn't we think that about Casey and then all hell broke loose when we brought her home to a more stimulating environment including cats and horses?

That moment, the doors opened and both playpens in front of us filled with dogs. It was a cacophony of barks and whines and bellows, a blend of medium, large, and extra-large dogs. Most dogs quietly walked around the pen, sniffing the floor, but a few dogs seemed a bit more aggressive. One dog in particular propped his front paws on the barrier in front of us and barked at us ferociously. He was so intense I noticed I was holding my breath. Dusty was not affected at all. He was curled up next to me on the sofa, his head and front paws in my lap, snoozing. David and I exchanged a look… this adoption was a done deal. I faxed the paperwork to Caitlin, paid the adoption fee, and moments later we were on the Massachusetts turnpike heading home. Dusty snuggled between us on the middle seat of the truck as if he had lived with us all his life.

"I don't think Dusty is a great name." I looked at David, "It's not aspirational, who wants to be dusty?" I liked names that expressed the personality of a dog, or something that related to the life or lifestyle of the family. We talked about Patches because of the brown patch covering the right side of his face. But it didn't roll easily off the tongue. How about Gunner?" David asked.

I thought it had too much of a hunting dog connotation.

When David and Dusty fell asleep in the truck, I continued through the gamut of possible names: Tango, cute but not relevant. Pirate, fitting considering the patch, but awkward to call, Pi-rate!

I imagined us in schools teaching kids about compassion and boundaries, and I wanted the name to make sense. Somehow that brought to mind the Eagle Scouts; I always envisioned them in their khaki uniforms gazing at the world through telescopes. Looking at this pup with his brown patch over his right eye brought that visual home. And Dusty also looked a lot like my first horse named Scout, who was white with brown spots. Immediately I thought of a blog I could write from the perspective of this new pup—seeing the world through his eyes; I'd call it "Scoutin' Around" and it would be full of our adventures on the road.

When David woke up, I asked him what he thought about the name Scout. He loved it, and so Dusty became Scout.

Fortunately, the cats and horses accepted Scout from the get-go. A week later when we finally moved into our home in Vermont all the animals had to establish new routines and discover new hangouts. All were on even ground.

Scout adapted well. At first he was shy and a little bit scared around our horses Shana and Cutter and the goat

Sammy, but within a couple of weeks Scout's personality began to shine through. On a hot summer day he joined me during barn chores. While I stuffed hay bags in the hay shed, Scout ran around, exploring the run-in barn. Suddenly, I heard a big splash. When I looked out the door Scout was sitting in the big, pink, horse-water bucket.

A few weeks later, Scout figured out how he could be helpful. After dropping the horse feed into Shana's and Cutter's feeders, I put the small grain buckets in front of the barn. Scout snuck up on the buckets, grabbed one and took off toward the house. Encouraged by me telling him to "bring the bucket to the house" Scout dropped the first bucket near the front door and came back for the second. Nowadays he's the official bucket carrier.

We quickly learned that Scout needed additional jobs to keep him happy and engaged. So, now we ask him to bring hay bags out to the horses and to pick up sticks in the field. If we don't give him jobs, he will come up with his own ideas and that involves 'stealing' things and burying them in random flowerbeds.

We have also learned that Scout is incredibly kind, committed, and loving, and that he is, like all other animals, an effective and patient teacher. Watching him develop into a beautifully attentive and hard-working farm dog made me face the reality that he's not really interested in being the traveling ambassador to share our work with people and animals around the world. Scout gets nauseous in the car and he can't stand being leashed and brought into small or crowded spaces.

As of right now, what Scout needs is to roll around on the grass, run through the fields, and find jobs on the farm. That means I'm putting my vision on the back burner. Accepting and embracing Scout for who he is in the moment allows him to develop into the dog he was always intended to be. And I can't wait to learn more about him.

Thank You

I've been down many roads, worked with, talked to, and learned from a lot of people, and in the end I've come back to where it all began.

For as long as I can remember, my parents have gotten a kick out of watching the birds in our backyard. It was astounding how aware my mother was of the goings-on around the bird feeder. I can hear her excited voice: "Oh, the robin is back. Yesterday the bullfinch threw him out of the feeder." Just like my mom once pointed out the particulars about the birds she had observed, I am now a keen observer of behavioral cues from humans and animals and have a deep awareness of nuances, both physical and energetic.

Following in the footsteps of my dad, who conducts research on absolutely everything before drawing conclusions, I too love to perceive, hypothesize, and then draw conclusions about the meaning of words, body postures, facial expressions, and energetic shifts emitted by people and animals.

I am grateful for the foundation my parents provided.

Many humans have taught me through example. Watching my former husband, John, staying fully attentive to our dog, Amber, the horses, and Flitzer was a reminder for me to approach them always from the heart, never just the mind.

Through their words and actions, others have reflected back to me that trusting my own and my animals' instincts was the most important lesson I had to learn.

Many people have supported my evolution and writing. My sweet sister backed me up every time I called to tell her my fears and doubts. And dear friends kept encouraging me to keep on keepin' on when I felt less than confident. The teachers and peers in my writing groups propelled my writing forward, and their feedback demonstrated the effects a well-told story can have. Yet only through the skillful guidance of my editors, Sarah Melcher and Suzanne Kingsbury, have I found the courage to bring these stories out into the world. Thank you!

I am so grateful to Kathy Lynch, founder and editor at *The Pet Gazette,* who offered me the column, and Cindy Thibault, the former publisher of *Pet Tails,* who asked me to write for her paper too. Stephanie Sanders, the publisher of *Massachusetts Horse,* gave me my first big writing job, a six-part series about Mindful Connections. I am so thankful for that life-changing opportunity. Maura Condrick, through your beautiful illustrations the stories and anecdotes in this book have come to life visually. I am so glad you said 'yes' to this project. I am grateful for Jeff Woodward who captured so much spirit in his heartfelt and beautiful photography. Big love to Margaret Wimberger and Kate Baldwin, my copy editors, and, to Martin Rouillard, my publisher at Smart Cat Publishing. Your collective support has made my publishing dream come true. You helped me give voice to the animals so they could be heard.

Which leads me to the heroes of my stories: the animals.

I am grateful for their presence, patience, and persistence.

I can feel the counsel of those who have passed and I am excited about the daily lessons of those around me. I finally understand and gladly accept my role as their ambassador. If I stay present they will continue to guide me on how to best do my job.

A special thanks to Jesse for leading me to my partner David. Because of David, unconditional love is something I experience not just with animals but also with another human.

If you are ready to add some pet logic to your life, head on over to my website: www.pet-logic.com. There you'll find photos and more anecdotes about Flitzer and friends, and several tools to create mindful connections in your life using the Mindful Connections Principles and the Mindful Connections Wheel. If you just want to drop me a line, email me at nicole@mindful-connections.com.

And, if you loved the stories for the stories' sake, I've got some good news for you. Turn the page and get a sneak peek of an upcoming book I am writing with my horse Shana. The working title is *Shana's Point of View*. She has yet to tell me more details.

Author's Notes

Until I met Shana, I had always nursed older, damaged, or misunderstood horses back to wellness—the ones who freaked out on crossties, suffered from laminitis, and required special care. I was particularly fond of those who had shut down because one too many times someone had "made" them behave. I was attracted to the horses who carried baggage. They made me feel needed. I had something to offer them.

Shana was different. This doe-eyed Arabian filly was born at a little farm in Upstate New York and had spent her first year without concern or worry. When she came to me as a yearling, I promised to do my best not to crush her spirit.

As the months went by and Shana learned to trust me, something miraculous happened, Shana started to talk to me. Sometimes she did this through her body and at other times she would send me thoughts. She eventually asked for her own book, and I figured, why not? I have learned a lot from her, maybe you will too. *Shana's Point of View* is one of the next books in the Pet Logic series. Shana and I thought we'd give you a little taste of her so you know what to look forward to. Enjoy!

PREVIEW

Shana's Point of View
How it Began

Before I get too philosophical right away, I need to share with you how it all started.

I knew change was in the air. I had overheard that some of the horses at the barn might be leaving.

Since there were only three of us, I wondered who was moving. Would it be Kaylaa, my favorite horse in the world—the one who took me under her wing when Mom left a few months ago? Or Jack, the other baby horse, who gets kind of fresh when Barbara plays with him? Or would it be me? I was born here at the barn and just celebrated my first birthday with everybody. This was all very worrisome.

Then one day two people came down the driveway toward the barn to look at the horses. I immediately poked my head through the open window of my stall door to check them out. Who were they here for?

The people greeted Kaylaa, my friend, the beautiful one. They stood near her stall door and talked to her. I stuck my little face around the corner to figure out what they were up to and heard them say, "She is so peaceful. " "What a profile! " "Look how pretty she is." Barbara took Kaylaa out of her stall and tied her in the aisle so the people could brush her. Then they put a saddle on her and asked Barbara to ride her. They seemed to like what they saw.

Next, the other woman got on Kaylaa and rode her around in the backyard. I could tell Kaylaa really wanted to go out on the trails and not just run around in circles in the backyard. Those small circles seem to bother her. I wondered if the lady noticed that Kaylaa was a little troubled. Either way, they seemed very interested in her.

When they came back into the barn Barbara asked if the people wanted to take two horses, Kaylaa and me. But the people said they did not have a stall for me. Nevertheless, Barbara showed me off. She removed my blanket so the people could see how pretty I am.

They liked me a lot; I could feel it. They said I looked like a doe with my warm, brown eyes. I felt nice when they said it.

A few weeks later the woman came back and picked Kaylaa up. The woman looked at me again and said how pretty and sweet I was with my fuzzy mane and forelock. And then Kaylaa left. I was stuck with the other horse. He was young like me, but he was a bully. He tried to push me around a lot, but I stood my ground, for the most part.

Nevertheless, the first few days without Kaylaa were really hard; I missed hanging out with her. I really missed her. Week after week I waited to see if anyone would come to pick me up. Barbara mentioned that a man from New Jersey who had liked my dad was interested in me. My dad is a famous show horse who wins all kinds of ribbons. The man wanted to get me so I could win lots of ribbons for him. I was not sure what that meant, but I guess I was up for anything. Anything was better than hanging out with my pushy neighbor.

But deep inside I was hoping the people who took Kaylaa changed their mind and would pick me up as well.

Of course you know already what came next. I wouldn't be writing this if they didn't come back for me.

CPSIA information can be obtained at www.ICGtesting.com
Printed in the USA
BVOW06s0842080216

435941BV00002B/3/P

9 781987 957587